ELEMENTS OF
Genealogical Analysis

ELEMENTS OF
Genealogical Analysis

Robert Charles Anderson, FASG

New England Historic
Genealogical society
AmericanAncestors.org

2014

ISBN-13: 978-0-88082-313-5
Library of Congress Control Number: 2014945040

Design/cover design by Carolyn Sheppard Oakley
Printed by King Printing Company, Lowell, Massachusetts

NEW ENGLAND HISTORIC
GENEALOGICAL SOCIETY
Boston, Massachusetts
AmericanAncestors.org

Contents

Preface

I have had this little book in mind for more than thirty years, and would like to record at this point my state of mind in the late 1970s and early 1980s, when it was first conceived. I was at that time quite new to genealogy, and had in the prior decade or so tried my hand at two other "careers," military intelligence and molecular biology. These two pursuits, seemingly quite distant from genealogy, provided both the basis for my genealogical skills and the impetus for the writing of a book on methodology.

First, in these two careers I developed the analytic tools that were to become very useful in my genealogical work. In my last two years of military service I spent most of my time studying radio-relay networks. By examining hundreds of radio messages, one amassed much data on the layout of the network, including perhaps a statement that Station A was next beyond Station B, or that Station D was between Station C and Station E. From such clues one eventually put together a picture of the entire relay network of radio stations.

My years in the world of molecular biology, during my last two years as an undergraduate and my two years as a graduate student, coincided with the first blossoming of rapid protein sequencing, and the very beginnings of rapid nucleic acid (DNA) sequencing. In the middle of my second year of graduate work I was asked by one of my professors to assist in the preparation of a problem-solving text for beginning biochemistry students. One of the problems included in this volume was a simplified recreation of the sequencing of insulin, the first successful sequencing of a long strand of amino acids, and the prelude to the burst of protein sequencing soon thereafter. Protein sequencing was carried out by the application of a battery of digestive enzymes to the protein. Each enzyme attacked the amino acid sequence of the protein in a different place, and so each enzyme produced a different collection of fragments of the protein. By studying these fragments, and the ways in which they overlapped, one was able to reconstruct the full sequence of the protein.

Both of these analytic techniques proceed by gathering bits of fragmentary data, comparing one bit to another, and eventually building up a complete picture of the entire structure that one wished to describe. I have found that these same procedures, with some obvious modifications, transfer well to the study of genealogy, and perhaps as you read through this book you will see how my experiences in military intelligence and molecular biology have helped me in doing genealogy.

Second, in both military intelligence and molecular biology (or almost any other organized intellectual discipline that you might name), one finds a wide range of comprehensive and up-to-date reference works. These might include finding aids, such as dictionaries or bibliographies, and methodological texts, such as cryptographic guides or laboratory manuals. Genealogy, largely because it does not have substantial financial support from large institutions, lacks many of these reference works. In the case of colonial New England research, the basic reference work was still James Savage's *Genealogical Dictionary of New England*, which had been published during the Civil War. The increasing obsolescence of this and other similar reference works drove my thinking in developing the Great Migration Study Project.

At the same time, I noted that most of the existing manuals describing how to do genealogical research were heavily weighted toward the discussion of sources and where to find them, with relatively little attention devoted to the methods of analysis of the sources and records or of the procedures for solving genealogical problems. By the early 1980s I had formulated the two Fundamental Rules of Genealogy (see the next section of this volume, *Overview*). In 1982, at the Second Annual Conference in the States of the National Genealogical Society at Indianapolis, Indiana, Neil D. Thompson, FASG, and I jointly presented a session entitled "Evaluating Evidence." In my portion of the lecture I set forth publicly for the first time the two Fundamental Rules and some associated ideas, which are now the core of the present volume. In 1984 some of this material was used in the first edition of *The Source: A Guidebook of American Genealogy*, in the section titled "Introduction to Genealogical Records and Techniques," and at about the same time I employed some of the same material in my lectures at the National Institute on Genealogical Research at the National Archives in Washington, D.C.

The system of solving genealogical problems which grew out of those ideas from the early 1980s, and which is elaborated in the chapters to follow, has served me well over the last quarter of a century in my work on the Great Migration Study Project.

RCA

Acknowledgments

Alvy Ray Smith, FASG, and David E. Rencher read the entire manuscript and made valuable suggestions and comments. Alvy also deployed his computer graphics expertise in improving the problem-solving sequence diagram and in other areas.

Four of my colleagues, all Fellows of the American Society of Genealogists, discussed with me work that they had previously done and which I was able to employ in the examples and case studies: David C. Dearborn, Patricia Law Hatcher, James L. Hansen, and Gale Ion Harris.

My thanks to the Winslow Farr Sr. Family Organization for permission to use the material on Stephen Farr in Chapter Five.

At the New England Historic Genealogical Society, it seemed at times that the entire staff was assisting in producing this book. I have had strong support throughout from top management: Brenton Simons, Tom Wilcox, and Ryan Woods. Penny Stratton and Leslie A. Weston have assisted at all stages. Several other NEHGS staff members also read the entire manuscript at various stages and provided many useful and important comments: Scott C. Steward; Ginevra Morse; Lynn Betlock; Henry B. Hoff, FASG; David C. Dearborn, FASG; Helen S. Ullmann, CG, FASG; Suzanne Stewart; and Kristin Britanik. Ginevra Morse used her many skills to turn my rough ideas for linkage bundle diagrams, dossier diagrams, and chart pedigrees into works of art, and Carolyn Sheppard Oakley designed the interior and the cover.

Thanks also are due to copyeditor Silvia Glick, production artist Anne Lenihan Rolland, and indexer Steve Csipke.

Overview

Elements of Genealogical Analysis is a book about how to solve genealogical problems. As the director of the Great Migration Study Project, which examines all people who migrated from England to New England in the years between 1620 and 1640, I have developed a strict methodology that has helped me establish complete genealogical definitions of the people I have treated. Although my expertise is in early New England, and the examples in this book derive from that place and era, you can adapt these methods to solve genealogical problems in any time period and geographic area.

You must be rigorous and methodical in your research. Whether you are investigating a person who left England in 1620 or an ancestor who left Eastern Europe in 1900, you need to attend to the substance and the reliability of records and sources. After all, all of us who are researching people in the past are focused on the same thing: developing a list of reliable information about a particular person. We have all struggled with unreliable genealogies written by people who have made quick assumptions that a particular record refers to their ancestor—incorporating a record that seems relevant without carefully assessing the dates and the surrounding information, including details of other names in the records. By using the methods I outline in this book, you will avoid making such mistakes.

A key part of this methodology involves making yourself familiar with the sources in a particular time and place and with the kinds of records available in a particular time and place. Whereas it is beyond the scope of this book to provide that kind of historical detail for every possible genealogical problem you might encounter, you will learn what you need to know about the sources and records you do encounter.

The purpose of this book is to elaborate a systematic methodology for doing genealogy. Specifically, this book will look at how to solve a genealogical problem. Each genealogical problem really comes down to one basic question: does a given record or piece of evidence refer to the person I am researching? You will look at the steps necessary to come to a solution of that problem, which might be very easy in some cases and very difficult in others.

I have developed this problem-solving system by analyzing a wide range of books and articles written by many of the most prominent genealogists, extracting elements common to all of these researchers, and arranging the steps in a logical sequence. This method attempts to take into account all the steps required for the solution of the easiest or the most difficult genealogical problem. I have also analyzed my own past genealogical work, both as part of the Great Migration Study Project and elsewhere. Drawing on my own personal experiences may seem a bit immodest—but, after all, any genealogist is much more aware of his or her own thought processes than those of another.

Fundamental Rules Of Genealogy

This comprehensive methodology can be formulated as two compact, fundamental rules.

First Fundamental Rule: All statements must be based only on accurately reported, carefully documented, and exhaustively analyzed records.

Second Fundamental Rule: You must have a sound, explicit reason for saying that any two individual records refer to the same person.

Much is packed into these two rules, but there is a very important reason for having two and only two rules. The First Rule considers the validity and accuracy of individual records before any genealogical judgments are made. The Second Rule concerns itself totally with the process of combining records and drawing conclusions. Stated more briefly: the First Rule deals with evidence and the Second Rule deals with proof.

In implementing the Fundamental Rules, two complementary sets of procedures guide us: analytic tools and a problem-solving sequence. A problem-solving sequence provides an orderly road map guiding you from your first step in tackling any genealogical problem until you eventually reach a satisfactory conclusion. Cutting across all the steps of this sequence, a set of analytic tools helps handle both the evidence and the proof. Since they apply at all stages of the problem-solving sequence, let's look at the analytic tools first.

Part One: Analytic Tools

Before taking a step-by-step tour through the problem-solving sequence, you need to know something about the various analytic tools that you will use over and over again, at every step of the process. The three tools set forth here are **source analysis**, **record analysis**, and **linkage analysis**. The first and second of these tools examine and evaluate the evidence you have collected, in preparation for the application of the third tool, which takes you to your genealogical conclusions.

Source analysis [Chapter One] is the detailed examination of a **source** (a coherent group of **records** created by a single jurisdiction or a single author for a defined purpose), such as a diary, the census for a given year, the probate records of a given jurisdiction, or the marriage records of a church. At this stage, you are not looking for data on an individual person, but for information on the "how" and "why" of the source's creation—information that will later help you interpret specific records within that source.

Record analysis [Chapter Two] is the detailed examination of a **record** (the portion of a **source** that pertains to a single event) from within a source, such as a diary entry, a census enumeration for a family, a will, or a record of a specific marriage. Using your knowledge of the source gained during the **source analysis** stage, you extract as much as possible from this record, *before* proceeding to **linkage analysis**.

Linkage analysis [Chapter Three] examines two or more exhaustively analyzed records that potentially refer to the same person and attempts to determine whether the records should be ascribed to a single individual, or whether they pertain to two or more individuals. A possible result of this analysis is that there is not yet enough information to determine linkage.

Note that **source analysis** and **record analysis** implement the third element of the First Fundamental Rule, which calls for "exhaustively analyzed records," while **linkage analysis** is a lengthier way of stating the Second Fundamental Rule

Part Two: Problem-Solving Sequence

The problem-solving sequence is a coordinated series of five steps that will take you from question to answer. These five steps are represented graphically in Figure 1, in a manner that helps you to be constantly mindful of the Fundamental Rules, and of the core distinction between evidence and proof.

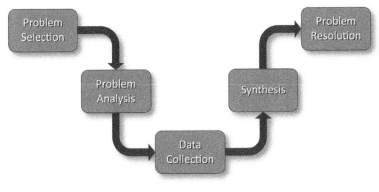

Figure 1.

1. **Problem selection** [Chapter Four]: What is the specific genealogical question? Are you attempting to identify the spouse of some person you are interested in, or do you want to establish a parent-child relationship? More complicated problems than these can be imagined, but, as you will see, your work is simplified if you break larger projects into smaller pieces. In this step you are usually looking at genealogical conclusions previously made by you or by other researchers, and choosing just where to review or extend this work. You are, then, looking at records that have already been linked together to define one or more individuals. Figure 1 represents this step at an elevated level, indicating that the material under consideration does not consist of isolated records, but represents a higher-level construct, derived from some genealogist's judgment.

2. **Problem analysis** [Chapter Five]: In problem analysis, you collect and examine what you already know about the problem, both to search out erroneous assumptions and conclusions in your (or others') prior work, and to determine what new data you must find. You pick apart that prior work; you undo, at least provisionally, the linkage work done by previous genealogists; and you take the problem back to its basis in the records more or less contemporaneous with the events themselves. In other words, you employ **reverse linkage analysis**. For this reason, this step appears at an intermediate level in Figure 1, to show that you are moving from a group of linked records back to the stage of isolated, unlinked records.

3. **Data collection** [Chapter Six]: Following up on the results of your previous analysis, you search for new records, or reexamine records already obtained during earlier research. During this step in the sequence, special attention is paid to the first two elements of the First Fundamental Rule, that all records must be "accurately reported" and "carefully documented." This phase of research differs from place to place and time to time, and has been the subject of many excellent publications. Thus although data collection is an important step, we do not spend a great deal of time on the topic in this book.

4. **Synthesis** [Chapter Seven]: Having identified any records that were consulted during the creation of prior genealogical conclusions relating to the problem under study, and having collected new records pertaining to the same problem, you first subject them to **source analysis** and **record analysis**. Then you apply **linkage analysis** to this collection of records, either to confirm previous conclusions or to arrive at a new solution. This step is shown in Figure 1 at an intermediate level, indicating that you are working from the lower level of isolated records to a higher plateau in which you have synthesized these records into a solution to your problem.

5. **Problem resolution** [Chapter Eight]: As you proceed with the **linkage analysis**, you monitor your work of synthesis, to see when it suggests that you have reached a conclusion, and then you test that conclusion. As the diagram shows, you have

now returned to the level from which you started, the level of genealogical conclusions. If you have done your work well, your conclusions will be more robust than those from which you began.

Although these five steps are presented as sequential and distinct, it is natural for the human brain to jump around and consider aspects of the problem simultaneously and/or out of this order. But when confusion or uncertainty arises, this list of specific steps provides a solid foundation to which to return, to make sure you're on the right track. The system is meant to serve as a checklist to assist you when you go astray.

Since any or all of the three analytic tools described above may be used at each step of the problem-solving sequence, Part One of this volume comprises chapters for each of the tools, so that they will be available to you in Part Two, which presents the five steps of that sequence.

Having explained what this book is, or is intended to be, let me now say what it is *not*. First, this system is not necessarily the only possible system. Quite likely dozens of different systems might be developed by following the basic steps of genealogical research, any one of which would be successful. The important point here is that you will learn at least one comprehensive system.

Second, I do not contend that any of the elements in this system is new, or that the system will magically provide solutions to problems that have resisted the attacks of generations of genealogists. What is new here is the arrangement into a comprehensive program.

Third, although most of the examples presented in this volume are from colonial New England, the proposed system is not limited to any one time or place. Different eras and different regions will give rise to different sorts of records and to different local laws and customs. All of this will affect the way in which you analyze and interpret individual records, but it does not change the sequence of steps needed to solve genealogical problems, nor does it alter the general principles of problem resolution.

PART ONE
Analytic Tools

Chapter One

Source Analysis

Before you begin to work your way through the basic problem-solving sequence, presented in Part Two of this volume, you need to be familiar with the analytic tools that will be applied at all steps of that sequence. The first two of these tools, explained in this chapter and the next, are closely related to one another: **source analysis** and **record analysis**. These two tools implement the third element in the First Fundamental Rule: "All statements must be based only on . . . exhaustively analyzed records." Before proceeding to these analytic steps, it is necessary to define **source** and **record**.

Definition of Source and Record

A **source** is a coherent collection of **records** created by a single jurisdiction or a single author for a defined purpose.

A **record** is that portion of a **source** which pertains to a single event.

Genealogists utilize an enormous range of source material, including probates and deeds, records of vital events, court proceedings, ship passenger lists, church registers, and many more. Here are just a few examples of source types of interest to genealogists:

The registers of a church. In some times and places church registers record all events—whether baptisms, marriages, or burials—in a single sequence, whereas other churches will maintain separate registers for each type of event. In some instances it may be possible to determine which ministers or other church officials created different parts of the registers, in which case it may be appropriate to designate the work of these different scribes as distinct sources.

A census. A census might be only a few sheets of paper enumerating the families in a single town. At the other end of the spectrum would be the modern census of a nation state, such as one of the decennial U.S. censuses. Counting the federal census as a single source may work or may not, depending on how consistent the census takers' criteria were. On the one hand, as long as consistent criteria were employed in creating the census, calling the 1840 census for the United States a single source could be a reasonable position to take. In those censuses where the census enumerator may be identified, however, the set of entries gathered by any one enumerator could be called a source, given that different enumerators often interpreted their instructions differently.

A cemetery. In general, a cemetery should be considered a single source. Each cemetery has its own reason for being, and so the styles on tombstones—and other features of the burial process and recordkeeping—may differ from place to place. Moreover, when a very large cemetery has distinct sections, each section should probably be considered a separate source.

A private diary. The private writings of an individual about his or her own life, whether limited to a single event, such as a trip around the world, or spread over many decades of a lifetime, constitute a single source. Even if the diary is recorded in several volumes, the single authorial voice makes it a single source, assuming reasonable continuity.

The Analytic Approach

Over the years many different schemes have been proposed for analyzing gene-alogical sources and records. The method presented here is a literary-historical approach. The main mode of analysis will be the particular version of that approach developed by the discipline of diplomatics. (See Appendix B, "The Three Paradigms," for discussion of other modes of analysis, and the reasons for choosing among them.) The strategy of diplomatics is to pose a series of questions to each source (and then later to the records of interest within that source), with the goal of determining the **substance** and **reliability** of the material you will eventually use to build your genealogical conclusions.

> **Substance** consists of the various statements of fact presented by a given source or record: the names, dates, places, and relationships that will be of value to you when you come to the business of linking two or more records together.
>
> **Reliability** means the relative value of each of these facts when making linkage decisions. In other words, when you have two or more records that disagree on the same factual point, how do you decide which (if any) should be given preference?

Source analysis generally precedes **record analysis**. In order to maximize your understanding of the substance and reliability of any record, you must first understand that record within the context of its source. Different jurisdictions, for example, will handle probate differently. Different clerks will have distinctive styles in recording vital events. The examples given in this chapter and the next will attempt to explain these variations. (On occasion a result obtained during record analysis teaches you something new about the source, and leads you to circle back to the source analysis stage, or vice versa. An example of this dialectical interaction among the analytic tools will be seen below in the discussion of **list analysis**, a subset of source analysis.)

In this book we deliberately avoid the use of the word "document" as much as possible when discussing genealogical evidence. This word generally connotes a physical object in a way that source and record, as conceived here, do not. A source may consist of a single document, such as a genealogical sampler created by a young girl in the nineteenth century. On the other hand, a source may comprise a roomful of documents, such as the probate records of a single jurisdiction. Likewise, a record may be a single document, as with a deed, or it may be a boxful of documents, as with the probate papers associated with the estate of one individual.

Questions Addressed To Genealogical Sources

The list of questions posed in this chapter and the next does not exhaust the full range of questions that might be asked. Different sources will present different problems, and so each source that you work with may require an adjustment to the set of relevant questions. The questions below are those that are most frequently pertinent to your genealogical concerns.

1. Is it the original or a copy?

An important element in determining the **reliability** of a source, and therefore of the records within that source, is whether the version being examined is the "original," a copy, or even a copy of a copy. (The word "original" is in quotes because, although we may not always be able to identify a given version of a source as being the earliest created, we should be able to decide between two versions of a source which is earlier and which is later, the earlier generally being the more reliable.)

The resolution of this problem bears directly on the question of the **reliability** of the source being studied. In 1949 Claude Shannon, a pioneer in information and communications theory, "published an important theorem which states, in essence, that information cannot be transmitted over long periods of time without experiencing some deterioration in quality due to 'noise' in the copier process."[1] It is important to be alert for the signs of this "deterioration . . . in the copier process," this relentless consequence of the Second Law of

Thermodynamics, wherein disorder and error increase every time a **source** or **record** is replicated.

Multiple copies of a given source may exist for many reasons. As older bound volumes of records are damaged by extensive use, custodians of those records may arrange for copies of those volumes to be created many years after the records therein were originally entered, sometimes centuries later. With court records especially, multiple copies may be needed if a case pertains to two or more jurisdictions, or if required for an appeal.

(A consideration that arises occasionally at this early point in the analysis of a source is whether you may be dealing with a forgery. Fortunately, this problem appears relatively rarely in genealogical research, but you must always be alert for forged documents. In order to avoid wasting time and energy in analyzing forged material, this problem should be addressed at the earliest stages of the analytic process. Two examples of forgeries of genealogical significance are given in Appendix D.)

▶ Example One: Vital Records

In 1980, when David Curtis Dearborn, FASG, longtime reference librarian at New England Historic Genealogical Society, was exploring his Curtis ancestry, he encountered a discrepancy in the published vital records of Salem, Massachusetts.[2] William Curtis, the earliest identified progenitor in this line, married Anna Smith at Salem on 31 December 1692, but the date of birth for their eldest known child, daughter Mary, was given as 11 May 1692, nearly eight months before the date of the marriage. The published vital records for most Massachusetts towns, while generally reliable, have the defect of having been rearranged in alphabetical order, regardless of the sequence in which the events were originally set down in the town record books. So a visit to the office of the Salem city clerk was in order.

When David arrived at that busy office and stated his problem, one of the clerks disappeared into the vault and returned with the published Salem vital records, the very source that had presented the problem in the first place. David very patiently explained the problem in further detail, and pointed out that what he really wanted to see was the "original" of the vital records. The clerk made a second trip into the vault and this time returned with a ledger-sized volume, which turned out, upon inspection of the handwriting, to be a nineteenth-century copy of the early town vital records. This was an improvement, because the copy set forth the records not in alphabetical order, but arranged by families, a frequent practice in early New England towns.

Still, this was not satisfactory, and David repeated his plea, with more specificity. The clerk then made a third trip to the vault and returned with a smaller, older volume. The entries were arranged as in the later transcript, by families, but the ink and the handwriting were clearly from the late seventeenth or early eighteenth century. Each page had the information for two or three families, arranged in chronological order within each family. Inspection of the William Curtis family, and of several other families, revealed that all the entries dated before 1705 appeared to be in the same hand and the same ink, but that later entries were appended to each family at a later date, probably as they were brought in for recording, with differences in handwriting and ink. Apparently, then, the book was initially compiled in or about 1705 and augmented regularly for some years thereafter.

The question naturally arose, was this finally the "original," or was there yet an earlier version on which the 1705 volume was based? Or did the town clerk in 1705 go about the town, family by family, collecting the data to create this "original" volume? One more trip by the clerk into the vault did not reveal an earlier volume (which is not to say that such a volume never existed). Figure 1.1 presents a "pedigree" of the different versions of this source.

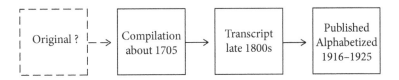

Figure 1.1. "Pedigree" of a Source.

The upshot of all this probing is that the dates for the marriage of William Curtis and the birth of his first child were correctly transcribed in the published version, and so the discrepancy in dates remained. But the exercise in tracking the source back in time was not without value. If the town clerk did go about in 1705 collecting dates from each family, the possibility arises that either the date of marriage or the date of birth of the first child, by 1705 more than a decade in the past, was misremembered or misrecorded, and that no one involved noticed the problem.

Example Two: Census Records

In 1850, 1860, and 1870, the United States Census Bureau created more than one copy of a given census enumeration: a federal copy; a state copy; and a county copy.[3] In such instances, when more than one version of a source exists, the researcher should attempt to examine all versions, as one never knows what will turn up. On occasion, the available versions may be so discrepant as to require further research.

James L. Hansen, FASG, has analyzed a case from the 1850 census of Sauk County, Wisconsin, in which "a series of entries . . . seems to list two individuals twice on the same page." This set of entries was found in the state copy, which led Hansen to examine the federal copy, where he found that the two households in question were entered quite differently.[4] (In this instance, the county copy apparently no longer exists.)

Hansen found that the federal copy made more sense than the state copy, both on direct inspection and by comparison with independent records for these families. To carry out this comparison, he collected further information on the family from Sauk County marriages, a Sauk County history, and inscriptions in a cemetery in Baraboo, Wisconsin.

Hansen concluded that in this instance, the federal copy was more accurate than the state copy (although this does not necessarily mean that the latter was copied directly from the former). Clearly, though, the clerk who produced the state copy was careless in his work, and this needs to be taken into account when consulting this version of the census. Note, however, that the surviving federal copy need not always be the more reliable; in other jurisdictions the copying process might produce a different set of errors.

Example Three: Church Records

One of the most important sources for English genealogy, from the sixteenth century to the present, has been the parish registers, containing baptisms, marriages, and burials performed in a given church. From an early date, the Church of England required that once a year each parish should produce a copy of the entries from their register for the preceding twelve months and submit that copy to the bishop of the diocese.

These so-called Bishop's Transcripts have not survived for all years for all parishes, but when they do they have great value. Most importantly, when the parish register itself has not survived, the Bishop's Transcript may be the only version of a vital event available to us. Even when the parish register does survive, there may be problems with legibility or interpretation of the date, which may be resolved by examining the Bishop's Transcipt.

Of course, since the Bishop's Transcript has been copied from the earlier entries in the register, we must always be alert for the possibility of a copying error. David Dearborn encountered just such a problem when researching his descent from the Wray family of Lincolnshire. David descends from Mark Wray, who had been born at Appleby, Lincolnshire, in 1747. In 1977 David found in the International Genealogical Index the baptisms of seven children of Mark Wray at Burton-upon-Stather, Lincolnshire, but no marriage for Mark Wray. This material had been extracted from the Bishop's Transcript for that parish; the parish register itself had not yet been microfilmed.

By 1991 the Burton-upon-Stather parish register had been filmed and was available at the Family History Library in Salt Lake City. When David read this film, he found the marriage on 9 January 1771 of Mark Wray and Margaret Eastwood. Comparison of the parish register with the Bishop's Transcript showed that the former contained the records of three marriages, while the latter had only two. In the copying process, one marriage, that for David's ancestor, had been lost.

Example Four: Marriage Records

Asa Brainerd was one of the first superstars of professional baseball. From 1868 to 1870 he was pitcher for the Cincinnati Red Stockings, the first avowedly professional team in the sport. Long-established baseball lore stated that Brainerd married Mary Truman soon after arriving in Cincinnati, but that he "deserted her when the Red Stockings disbanded after the season of 1870, leaving her virtually destitute and burdened by the necessity of raising their infant son, Truman Brainerd."[5] Examination of contemporary records tells a different story.

The *Cincinnati Daily Gazette* for 25 January 1871 reported that "Asel Brainard" and "Mary T. Truman" were married in that city on 23 January 1871. Brainerd did not acquire his wife upon arrival in Cincinnati, but three years later, after he had completed his career with the Red Stockings and was on the verge of moving back to play with the Washington team.

The next step was to obtain the official city recording of this marriage. As it happens, the early Hamilton County, Ohio, marriage records were lost to fire. The city officials attempted to replace these lost records by collecting information from a variety of sources, thus compiling a synthetic substitute for the early marriage records. These reconstituted records show that on 23 January 1871, "Asel Brainard" married "Mary Thompson Winn." Was the newspaper wrong? Had Mary perhaps been married earlier, to a man named Winn?

The marriage return recorded by the city was signed by "Thos. S. Yocom," Minister of the Gospel. The newspaper account stated that the couple were married by "the Rev. Thomas S. Yocom, Rector of Christ Church." A copy of the appropriate page from the marriage registers of Christ Church, Cincinnati, was obtained; this gave the names of groom and bride as "Asel Brainard" and "Mary Thompson Truman." The hand employed by the creator of the church register was neat and rounded, and the first three letters of the bride's surname could be read on a careless glance as a capital "W," which might have led the scribe who was collecting the information for the city's reconstruction of the marriages to read the surname as "Winn" rather than "Truman." Judging only from the single photocopied page of the church register, all the entries, spread over more than a year, seem to have been made at the same time, so the church register itself may not be the "original."

Here is a situation in which the original of the city record has been lost and the church record may be a copy. Fortunately, the newspaper account is available to assist in resolving the discrepancy.

Example Five: Birth, Baptismal, and Probate Records

Benajah MacKall was born at Marshfield, Massachusetts, on 9 August 1712 and died at New London, Connecticut, before 6 November 1753, intestate. His eldest child, a daughter, was baptized at the Goshen church in Lebanon, Connecticut, on 13 February 1736/7, as "Faith Mackall." Elizabeth Pearson White, in her treatment of this family, tells us that "In Windham, Ruth was called 'Faith.' In Lebanon she was called 'Ruth.'"[6]

The reality was not as White described it. Two sets of records bear on this problem, both of which are relevant to the question of whether we are dealing with the original or a copy. First are the birth and baptismal records. The contemporary copy of the baptismal register for Goshen church in Lebanon has an entry for "Faith Mackall," dated 13 February 1737. The entries in this register occur in chronological order, and inspection of surrounding entries shows that this date should be interpreted as 13 February 1736/7.

The quickest way to check the town vital records for Connecticut towns is to examine the Barbour Index, an alphabetical compilation of most early surviving records, available as a card index for the whole state and as individual volumes for each town. Inspection of the Lebanon volume reveals this entry under the surname "McCall, Mackall":

Ruth, [d. Benajah & Hannah], b. Feb. 12, 1736/7, Vol. 1, Page 198

"Vol 1, Page 198" refers to the first volume of Lebanon town records that contains vital records. This survives in a nineteenth-century copy, where one finds the following entry on page 198:

Benajah Mackall & Hannah Otis were married
November the 6th A.D. 1735
Faith Mackall was born February 12th 1736/7

These two items were immediately followed by the birth records for two more children of Benajah and Hannah, son Nathaniel and daughter Delight. In Lebanon, then, the town clerk entered the vital records family by family, and chronologically within the family, rather than compiling a single chronological list for all births regardless of family, as was done in other towns.

The creator of the Barbour Index incorrectly read "Faith" as "Ruth." In the surviving nineteenth-century version of the town records, "Faith" is fairly clear, but one can see how it might be misread as "Ruth." But at this remove we do not know whether the indexer was using the eighteenth- or the nineteenth-century version of this record.

At any rate, basing our conclusion only on the birth and baptismal records, we see that the best versions available for these two sources agree that the given name of this child was "Faith."

The second set of records available to resolve this problem comes from the probate of Benajah's estate. Because Benajah MacKall owned land in more than one jurisdiction, his estate was probated in both the Windham and New London probate districts. (In Connecticut, the probate jurisdictions are not counties, but one town or a small number of towns.) As a result, at least four versions of the record of distribution of MacKall's estate (and an implied fifth version) have survived. In Windham District, we find among the loose papers in the probate file the record of the distribution of the estate of Benajah Mackall[7] and also the contemporaneously recorded copy in the probate register volume.[8] In New London District, we also find a probate file with a single loose paper, being the same record of distribution as in the Windham file,[9] and also a recorded copy in the probate register volume, which appears to be a nineteenth-century copy, the contemporaneous copy of the probate register no longer being available.[10]

The two surviving register volume copies of this record, as well as the implied contemporaneous register volume copy for the New London district, would have been copied from the loose file papers. But of the two file papers, which was the "original"? Comparison of the two file papers provides two strands of evidence that strongly point to the Windham version as the "original" from which the New London version was created.

On the Windham version the signatures of the three witnesses are different from one another and from the handwriting in the body of the distribution, whereas in the New London version the signatures of the three witnesses are all in the same hand, which is the same as the body of the text.

The docketing endorsements made by the probate clerk on the Windham version call the record "The Return of the Estate of Benajah Mackall deceased in Lebanon Exhibited 21 June 1758, Recorded August 1758," whereas the docketing information on the New London version says "Copy of the Division of the Real Estate of Benaja[h] Mackall of New London Deceased Lying in Lebanon, to be Recorded 12 June 1759," and also includes the docketing information from the Windham version, clearly establishing the priority of the Windham version.

Thus, the earliest version of this record of distribution available to us is the Windham file copy, from which two copies were made, one into the Windham probate register and one onto a separate sheet of paper for the New London probate files. The latter version was copied again, into the New London probate register, which itself was recopied in the nineteenth century. (See the accompanying sidebar on "Source Stemmata" for a graphic depiction of this sequence.)

Of the four surviving versions of this record, three give the child's name as "Faith." Only the nineteenth-century New London probate register volume differs, the name appearing as "Truth." Again, in agreement with the birth and baptismal records, the preferred name is clearly Faith. Again, the erroneous version of the name appears in a nineteenth-century copy of a missing eighteenth-century source. We cannot be sure when the error was made, but the unfamiliarity of the nineteenth-century clerk with eighteenth-century penmanship is the likely culprit.

Source Stemmata

The *Chambers English Dictionary* defines *stemma* as "a pedigree, family tree; a diagrammatic tree drawn up (using the internal evidence of manuscripts, etc.) to show the descent and relationships of the texts of a literary work." (*Stemma* being a word of Greek origin, the plural is *stemmata*.)

Given the immense number of early manuscript versions of the books of the Bible, scholars have created elaborate stemmata of these manuscripts to assist them in working out the history of variant readings of some passages. This technique has also been employed in the study of classical manuscripts, such as the plays of Euripides, which have come down to us in many versions.[11]

When you draw a pedigree chart in the course of your genealogical research, you are creating a *stemma* in the first sense of the dictionary definition. But the second meaning from the dictionary also comes into play in genealogical research, when you encounter a source or a record that survives in several different versions. The example of the multiple copies of the probate records of Benajah MacKall may be presented graphically as such a stemma, as shown in Figure 1.2.

The five versions of this one record are arranged in this four-generation stemma (or pedigree) on the basis of the analysis carried out in the main text [pages 8-10]. The ancestral record is the file paper from Windham Probate District. This was then copied twice, creating two second-generation versions: once into the Windham Probate District probate register and the second time as a loose paper for the New London Probate District file. The New London file copy was then recopied into the contemporary New London Probate District probate register, which cannot currently be located. Finally, sometime in the nineteenth century a transcript was made of the eighteenth-century register book, and here we find the deviant version of the name, in which "Faith" has become "Truth." Given the disappearance of the eighteenth-century version of the New London register book, it is impossible to tell whether the copying error was made between the second generation and the third, or between the third generation and the fourth

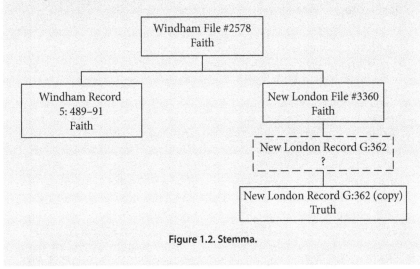

Figure 1.2. Stemma.

2. When was the source created?

Separate from the issue of whether we are dealing with the original or a copy is the distinction between the date or dates on which a source was first created and the dates of the events recorded within that source. If the source was created simultaneously with the recorded event or soon after, we would in general give more credence to such a source than one that covered the same events but was created long after the events so recorded. Here, as elsewhere, the issue is one of reliability.

The first example below, describing the journal that Governor John Winthrop of Massachusetts maintained between 1630 and 1649, speaks to this aspect of dating the creation of a source.

Moreover, on occasion we find a source that has no date of creation associated with it, or a highly dubious date. The second and third examples below describe a technique for ascribing a date of creation to some of these sources.

> ### Example One: Contemporaneous Records with Later Entries

John Winthrop resided in Massachusetts Bay from 1630 to 1649 and was governor of the colony for twelve of those years. Throughout his time in New England he maintained a journal, with regular entries, almost on a daily basis. Winthrop entered his journal in three separate volumes, covering respectively the years 1630–1636, 1636–1644, and 1644–1649. James Savage, a prominent antiquarian, prepared two editions of the journal, one published in 1825–1826 and the second in 1853. In 1825, after the completion of the transcription of all three original volumes, a fire in Savage's offices destroyed the original of the second volume.

In 1996 Richard S. Dunn and Laetitia Yeandle prepared a new edition of Winthrop's journal according to modern standards. They created a new transcription from the originals of the first and third volumes, but were, of course, forced to work from Savage's transcription of volume 2.[12]

In their preparation of the sections of the journal based on the original volumes 1 and 3, Dunn and Yeandle noted that in the 1630s most of Winthrop's entries were made within a few days or weeks of the events recorded, but there were many instances, indicated by differences in ink and in placement on the page, when Winthrop annotated some of these entries at a later date, sometimes years later. And by the 1640s many of his entries were made years after the events.[13] Obviously, we must treat these late entries differently from those made contemporaneously with the events themselves. If Winthrop was working from memory in making these annotations, the chance for inaccuracies in his statements was magnified. Also, since Dunn and Yeandle were not able to examine the original of the second volume, they were perforce unable to identify those spots where Winthrop made these belated entries, and we may be misled into believing that some entry made by Winthrop was created at the time of the event, when in fact it was generated some time later.

> ### Example Two: Comparing All Available Records

In 1903 John E. Stillwell discovered in the archives of the state of New York a seven-page document with the title "List of Inhabitants of the Towns of New Rochelle and Westchester," thought to be dated 1698.

Stillwell observed that in fact those names that he recognized were from Staten Island. Furthermore, by comparing the list with a handful of dates gathered mostly from secondary sources, he concluded that this document was actually created in 1706, and so published the list as "Census of Staten Island in the Year 1706." (Unfortunately, the document discovered by Stillwell was destroyed by fire in 1911, and all later analyses have had to rely on the transcription published by Stillwell in 1903.)

George E. McCracken was the next to examine this source. He sought out probate records and additional baptismal records for men whose names were given in the list, and concluded that the date of the document was 1708 or 1709. In 1999 Barbara Barth, in her study of the Van Woggelum family, arrived at a more complicated interpretation, concluding that different sheets of this source were compiled on different dates in 1707, 1708, and 1709.

In 2009 Patricia Law Hatcher, FASG, examined the list in much greater detail than had any of her predecessors. She noted that each of the early researchers had brought to bear on the problem only a limited number of the other records available for comparison. Pat considered a wide range of other sources and, within those sources, every record she could find for anyone in the list. In particular, she made extensive use of the baptisms from the Staten Island church (a source which had its own peculiar problems of interpretation).

Her method was to employ dates and ages from other sources and compare that information with the data found in the list under examination, with the goal of determining who should or should not have been on the list for a given date. For example, Yelis Ingart wrote his will on 2 January 1706/7 but was not on the list, so the census must have been compiled after 2 January 1706/7. Similarly, the will of Isaac Bellew was probated on 22 December 1709 and he was on the list, so the census must have been compiled before that date. By systematically and rigorously applying this logic to every available record, Pat continuously narrowed the window of dates within which the list could have been created and concluded that this census was taken "in late summer or early fall 1707, likely August or September 1707."[14]

Example Three: Using Independent Evidence

In the course of my work on the Great Migration Study Project, I came across a source similar to that analyzed by Pat Hatcher. In the early records of New Haven Colony is a lengthy list, three pages long in its printed version, which provided information on the estates of inhabitants of that jurisdiction. The list is undated, but, as published, falls between two other colony records for July of 1643. In 1967 Donald Lines Jacobus noted that "the list of planters and estates . . . was clearly drawn up as early as 1640–1, though copied into the records in 1643."[15] Jacobus did not provide the evidence behind his conclusion, but application of the same techniques employed by Hatcher supported and refined Jacobus's results.

The list included a column headed "Persons numbered," which set forth the household size at the time the list was generated. By studying several families for whom there is accurate independent evidence of family size, the date of the list could be placed between 17 November 1639 and 22 November 1640. Additional study of colony land grants and the deaths of male heads of household placed the creation of the list on or after 29 October 1640.[16]

Having obtained this date for the list, we can immediately use this information to analyze more of the entries. For example, Timothy Ford appears with a household of two, presumably Timothy and his wife, indicating that all of their surviving children were born after 1640, contrary to estimated ages for those children given in secondary sources. This is an instance of the dialectical relationship between source analysis and record analysis, in which we use individual, analyzed records from elsewhere in the dating of a source, and then use that newly obtained date to analyze a record within the source itself.

List Analysis

The second and third examples considered in answer to the question *When was the source created?* are examples of a subset of source analysis known as **list analysis**. For sources such as a census or a grant of lands, which are for the most part a list of names associated with perhaps one other piece of information, and for which the date is unknown or uncertain, list analysis aims to determine the date of the list, or the dates of the entries within the list. Such examination exemplifies the dialectical relationship between source analysis and record analysis, in which the benefits of detailed examination flow in both directions. The result obtained for the family of Timothy Ford in Example 3 is an instance of this two-way flow of analysis.

The following are the steps to be used in this process, exemplified by the Staten Island list studied by Pat Hatcher.

> 1. Search for as many reliable, dated individual records as you can find in other sources that pertain to the names in the list (in this case, baptismal records from a variety of churches, including the Staten Island church; and probate records, paying special attention to the date of the making and the date of the proving of the will).

2. Use these records to resolve the immediate problem of dating the source that contains the list (baptismal dates compared with ages on the list; dates of making and proving wills compared with who is and is not on the list).

3. After dating the list, consider that the flow of analysis may reverse direction: the date of the list may assist in interpreting records for other persons named in the list, a person or persons who may be of interest in a particular problem under investigation.

Many other examples of list analysis have been published in the *Great Migration Newsletter*. See, for example, Patricia Law Hatcher, "Members of the First Church of Roxbury," GMN 6:19-25; Melinde Lutz Sanborn, "Reverend James Allen's Church Census of 1688," GMN 7:3-6; [Robert Charles Anderson], "Rhode Island Freemen of 1655," GMN 10:9-10, 16; [Robert Charles Anderson], "Focus on Scituate" (dating a tax list), GMN 14:3-6; [Robert Charles Anderson], "Plymouth Men Able to Bear Arms," GMN 14:9-14.

3. Who created the source?

With the question *Who created the source?* the inquiry continues into the reliability of the source. If we are able to determine who created the source, we may be able to determine how accurate a reporter that person was. Perhaps evidence in the source itself will provide indications of unreliability, as when we encounter the unusual names in Rev. John Allin's church records, described in Example 1, below. We can then compare these names with other sources to confirm or refute our suspicions, and thus provide some guidance in utilizing this source. Or, as in the second example, we may observe significant differences in the way successive clerks carried out their duties in recordkeeping, in this case a set of town minutes. The next step is to set different values on the entries made by the two clerks. (Note that the question *Who created the source?* may generate a different answer than the question that we examine in the next chapter, *Who provided the information?*)

> ### Example One: Reliability of the Recorder

The town of Dedham, Massachusetts, was established in 1636. One year later the inhabitants began the process of founding a church. The first minister at Dedham, Rev. John Allin, in addition to maintaining a register of admissions to church membership and of baptisms, also wrote a detailed narrative of the tortuous process of founding the church.

As valuable as this source is for early New England church history in general, we find that Allin had some difficulty with names. For example, at one stage of the proceedings ministers from neighboring churches were consulted, among whom was "Mr. Madden teacher of the church in Dorchester."[17] This was, of course, Rev. Richard Mather, not Madden. A few years later, on 8 August 1639, "John Balducke the son of our sister Gay by her first husband was baptized."[18] As explained in a later chapter, this was John Borden, not Balducke.

With this knowledge in hand, we must always be alert while using the early Dedham church records for occasions when we encounter a name which doesn't seem to fit with records obtained from other sources. During the late 1630s, during the arduous task of selecting the seven founding members of the church, Allin refers three times to a man named "Thomas Morse," a name found nowhere else in early Dedham records.[19] These three records had led some genealogists to propose that Samuel Morse, a well-documented early Dedham settler, had an elder son Thomas, appearing only in these church entries. Careful examination of the life of Samuel Morse, however, revealed that these church records for a Thomas Morse actually pertained to Samuel Morse himself.[20]

For some reason, Rev. John Allin was not always a reliable reporter of the names of his congregants, and thus we must evaluate the Dedham church records created by this minister in a different light than the surviving records of most of the other early Massachusetts Bay churches.

Example Two: Personal Style of the Recorder

The town of Newbury, Massachusetts, was settled in 1635, and its surviving records of town proceedings commence on 10 June 1637. The first town clerk was John Woodbridge. On 19 November 1638, the town "ordered that Edward Rawson shall supply the place of Mr. Woodbridge & be the public notary and register [registrar] for the town of Newbury."[21]

John Woodbridge was Newbury town clerk for less than two years. In that period he produced more than thirty pages of detailed and carefully dated entries for town meetings and land grants. Once Edward Rawson took over the office, the nature of the surviving records changed drastically. Most of the entries are undated, except for the year, and for the most part only brief notices of land grants are included. There are no entries for town meetings as such and no evidence of who the town officers were during the years of Rawson's clerkship.

Just because there are no entries for town officers during Rawson's tenure does not mean there *were* no town officers. One possible way to fill this gap partially would be to consult the records for Essex County (within which

Newbury lay), as the town officers would on occasion appear at court to represent the town in some dispute. Such an item might appear in the court records many years after the time of service in the given office.

This difference between Woodbridge and Rawson most likely represents a difference in personal style between the two men, rather than a change in the way the town of Newbury did business. We should interpret early Newbury town records accordingly, analyzing town records as kept by Woodbridge differently than those kept by Rawson, in other words, considering them separate sources.

Similar situations will be seen with church records, where different ministers or clerks may enter baptisms, for example, differently. The earliest English parish registers, some dating from 1538, do not always name the parents of the child being baptized. Over time, the various persons making the entries might add the father's name, and then at an even later date, both the father's and mother's name. Each of these different arrangements requires a different mode of analysis; the less information provided in the record, the more effort required in distinguishing children of the same name, and in assigning the children to the appropriate family.

4. What formulas were used in creating the source?

Some, but not all, sources and records that genealogists encounter are organized according to a particular formula. This may be a particular pattern or regular sequence of required elements, or the repetitive use of the same block of verbiage in record after record in the same source. This commonly used language may be mere boilerplate, which you learn to ignore as you gain experience, or it may contain important clues to understanding the evidence, which you ignore at your peril.

The wording of a deed is an excellent example frequently encountered in genealogical work. A modern deed will usually have a regular sequence of elements, such as grantor, grantee, consideration, description of the property being transferred, and so on. But the English colonists of the seventeenth century were leaving a country in which the manorial system was in its dying days and freehold as a form of possessing land was on the increase. There were not yet fully developed registries for transfers of land in England, and the colonists had to invent such a system, with variations from colony to colony.

▶ Example One: Deeds

In the early deeds of Plymouth Colony, the following language frequently appears toward the end of the document:

> To be holden of our Sovereign Lord the King as of his Manor of East Greenwich in the County of Kent in free & common socage and not in

capite nor by knight's service. . . . It shall & may be lawful to and for the said Will[ia]m Wills either by himself or his attorney to record & enroll these presents or to cause them to be recorded & enrolled in His Majesty's court at Plymouth.[22]

This should not be interpreted to mean that the land in question, or the grantor or grantee, had anything to do with East Greenwich in Kent. The phrase "free & common socage" was an ancient English term meaning freehold, and the verbiage here simply indicates that that is the form of tenure of land conveyed, rather than one of the older feudal forms; "free & common socage" was regularly used by the Manor of East Greenwich.[23] The second phrase indicates that recording such a document in an official court register was encouraged, and by implication a relatively new practice.[24]

▶ Example Two: Mortgage Transactions

In early Massachusetts Bay Colony deeds, a mortgage transaction could look very much like a common sale unless one examines the legalese found toward the end of the deed. On 28 June 1652

> Robert Moone late of Boston in the Massachusetts, tailor, in consideration of a debt due to Theoder Atkinson of the same Boston, hatter, have bargained and sold and by these presents do bargain & sell, give, grant and alien, make over and confirm unto the said Theoder Atkinson my late dwelling house in the said Boston.[25]

At this point in the deed, it seems to be a garden-variety warranty deed, conveying all ownership. Many lines later, however, after the full description of the land and other language typical of a warranty deed, this passage appears:

> Provided always & it is hereby agreed & concluded upon with the said Theoder, that if myself, my heirs, executors or administrators shall pay unto the said Theoder . . . the full and just sum of forty-five pounds at or upon the first day of July [1654] . . . that then this bargain & sale to be surrendered & made void and of non-effect.

By this phrase, a warranty deed is converted to a mortgage. As much as we might like to skip over extensive tracts of seemingly innocuous formulaic and repetitive language in deeds, such an omission might be dangerous, as important information can be imbedded in such sections of the records.

In other sources, the formulas come not so much in the precise language as in the regular sequence of a limited number of required elements, as described below in the examination of the Winthrop Medical Journal.

In the following case studies, these source analysis questions are applied to two quite different sources. Because not every question necessarily applies to every source, our analysis will proceed somewhat differently from case to case. Later in the book, as we discuss more of the steps of genealogical analysis, we will revisit the two case studies in greater depth.

John Horne—Essex Quarter Courts

The manuscript records of the Essex County, Massachusetts, Quarter Courts for the seventeenth century, now housed at the Peabody Essex Museum in Salem, Massachusetts, may be divided into two broad classes: docket books and loose papers. The docket books are the chronological records of the matters brought before each sitting of the court. The loose papers comprise any documents that were submitted to the court bearing on matters under adjudication. (In addressing the questions below, we must consider the docket books and the loose papers separately.)

The records for this court from 1636 to 1686 have been published in nine volumes: *Records and Files of the Quarterly Courts of Essex County, Massachusetts* (Salem 1911–1975). The records from the docket books for each sitting of the court are given, with the contents of the loose papers appended as footnotes. Most of this material appears as abstracts.

Are the current manuscripts of the Essex Quarter Court records the originals?

For the dockets, the meaning of "original" can be somewhat slippery. Court clerks frequently made their initial entries in something called a "waste book," in which the proceedings and outcomes of court cases were written down in real time as the court was in session, without regard for the quality of the penmanship. Shortly after, usually within a few days, this material was then carefully copied over, by the same clerk, into a "fair copy," at which point the waste book might be discarded. Most of the surviving docket books are fair copies, but some of the waste books exist as well. When both versions exist, comparisons of the two copies may assist in resolving discrepancies or difficult readings.

The loose papers present many possibilities. Some documents, such as depositions, were created shortly before the date of the court at which the related case was heard. Other documents may be official copies taken from town records, in support of one side or another in a civil dispute. For example, in the second published volume of the Essex court records is a list of 1638 land grants for the town of Lynn, which is subscribed

"Copy taken from the town book of the records of Lynn, 10:1:1659–60 [10 March 1659/60], by Andrew Mansfeild, town recorder."[26] Such documents can be very valuable, in this case especially so, since the originals of the Lynn town records prior to 1691 have been lost. (If there are any forgeries in Essex Quarterly Court records, they are more likely to be found among the loose papers—where an individual appellant or defendant may have created a false document in support of his or her case—than among the docket books, which were created by the court clerks.)

When were the Essex Quarter Court records created?

As noted just above, the docket books were created at the time of the sitting of the court, at first perhaps as "waste books," and then the fair copies were usually made within a few days. The loose papers could have been created just before the sitting of the court at which the case was considered, or many decades earlier; each record must be analyzed for its date individually.

Who created the Essex Quarter Court records?

The docket books were created by the court clerks. The loose papers were created by a wide range of individuals, and must be evaluated on a case-by-case inspection.

Rachel Hart—Winthrop Medical Journal

Among the Winthrop Papers at the Massachusetts Historical Society is a manuscript of about a thousand pages known as the Winthrop Medical Journal. John Winthrop Jr. (1606–1676), son of Governor John Winthrop of Massachusetts Bay, maintained a record of his medical practice from 1657 to 1669. This stack of paper constitutes a source, for it was created by one man, for a single, well-defined reason, and covers a delimited term of years. This case study applies the questions outlined above to this source.

Is the current manuscript of the Winthrop Medical Journal the original?

Yes. The ink changes repeatedly throughout the source. Some entries are squeezed into small spaces, or written at right angles to the main entries. Nothing indicates that these pages were copied from an earlier, rougher version. This is the rough version.

When was the Winthrop Medical Journal created?

It was created from day to day, over the course of more than a decade, as John Winthrop Jr. met with and responded to his patients. Most of the entries were probably made in the comfort of his study at his home in Hartford, but in 1668 he was on a trip to Massachusetts Bay, during which he treated patients in Dorchester, Braintree, Rehoboth, and other towns. Apparently he had not brought the pages of his journal with him, or any blank paper, for he recorded his encounters with these patients in the blank spaces of a letter that he had received from Thomas Battelle of Dedham. No attempt was made to recopy these onto the usual, relatively neat pages.

Who created the Winthrop Medical Journal?

John Winthrop Jr. created it. All the entries, several thousand in number, are in the same handwriting, identifiable from other documents as that of John Winthrop Jr. The handwriting and the ink did, of course, change somewhat over the years of creation of this source. In fact, in some sections the ink must have been prepared improperly, for it has burned large holes in the pages, leading to the loss of much information. Nevertheless, this is clearly all the work of one man.

What formulas were used in creating the source?

Each entry follows a regular pattern: surname; given name; residence; age; relation to some other person; diagnosis; prescription. The age and relation to some other person do not always appear. In some cases the diagnosis was in Latin. The prescription generally used various apothecary symbols and other abbreviations. With the exception of the prescription, all these elements of a typical Winthrop entry will be used in the interpretation of individual records contained in later chapters.

Summary

In introducing our first analytic tool, **source analysis**, we began with two definitions:

A **source** is a coherent collection of **records** created by a single jurisdiction or a single author for a defined purpose.

A **record** is that portion of a **source** which pertains to a single event.

After presenting a few examples of types of sources according to this definition, we then proceeded to the process of **source analysis** itself, which consists of posing a series of questions to the source, with the goal of extracting from that source the maximum of information on **substance** and **reliability**.

Substance consists of the various statements of fact presented by a given source or record: the names, dates, places, and relationships that will be of value to you when you come to the business of linking two or more records together.

Reliability means the relative value of each of these facts when making linkage decisions. In other words, when you have two or more discrepant records that bear on the same factual point, how do you decide which (if any) should be given preference?

Although the list is not exhaustive, the questions researchers pose to the sources are:

- Is it the original or a copy?
- When was the source created?
- Who created the source?
- What formulae were used in creating the source?

Having discussed **source analysis**, the next step is to explore **record analysis**, the examination of individual records within a source.

Chapter Two

Record Analysis

Record analysis stands between **source analysis** and **linkage analysis**. In record analysis, the genealogist studies the record in the context of the source within which it exists, and then analyzes the record itself, attempting to extract from that record various conclusions that may be employed in the process of linkage with other records. As you proceed, you will encounter many examples of the reciprocal or dialectical relationships between the various pairs of categories of analysis.

Definition Of A Record

A **record** is the portion of a **source** that pertains to a single event.

Some examples of record types:

A baptism in a church register. A baptismal register will record dozens or hundreds of baptismal events. Some of them will be of interest to researchers if they apply to a given problem, and some will not. Having first studied the overall arrangement and mode of creation of a given register during source analysis, we now focus on one or more individual entries in that source.

A household in a census. As the census enumerator moves through a district, he or she attempts to visit all the residences. Whereas the enumerator is the creator of the census as a source, each household presents a different provider of information—perhaps the head of household, perhaps whoever was at home that day—and so each household becomes a separate record.

A tombstone in a cemetery. Some tombstones record a single event, the death of one person. Some tombstones provide evidence for the death of more than one individual. Whether a tombstone etched with the date of death for more than one person should be considered a single record or multiple records may depend on whether it is possible to determine when the tombstone was carved and also on whether some of the entries might be later additions.

An entry in a private diary. A single record within a diary might be the diarist's description of a single day, if the entry for that day is coherent and tells a single story, or it might be the recording of a single event, such as a celebratory meal or a business transaction.

Questions Addressed To Records

As in Chapter One, the goal in questioning each record is to ascertain the **substance** and **reliability** of the information in that record. The following list does not comprise every question that we might ask of a record, but it provides a useful framework. Note that the questions asked during record analysis may differ from those asked during source analysis.

1. When was the record created?

Determining the date of a record should always be one of the first steps in record analysis. Sometimes the dating in a source is clear, and there is a date associated with each entry, which you can simply read and interpret. But this is not always the case. Let's look at a few examples.

> **Example One: Missing Dates**
>
> Sometimes a source with many records on a page may have only a few dates associated with those many records. The earliest baptismal records for Salem, Massachusetts, contain the following typical sequence of records in the year 1638:[1]
>
> | | |
> |---|---|
> | 1:2 | Ezekiell, son of Ralph Fogge |
> | | Naomy, daughter of Francis Johnson |
> | 15:2 | Ann, daughter of Edmond Marshall |
> | 3:4 | Lyddea, daughter of John Black |
>
> Dates are given for three of the four names, but what is the baptismal date for Naomi Johnson? First, note that the early Salem church records have many entries with no dates directly associated with them. Second, it is apparent—not just from this handful of entries but from a broader examination of the source—that the dates are given as day followed by month. That is, 1:2 means the baptism took place on the first day of the second month. This is a good example of the dialectical relationship between source analysis and record analysis, for it is impossible to obtain the proper date for any of these baptisms from just one isolated record taken out of the context of the whole source.
>
> It is important to remember that in early New England, where the calendar year was taken to begin on 25 March [Lady Day], the first month

was March, the second was April, and so on to the twelfth or last month, February. Thus "1:2" is 1 April, "15:2" is 15 April, and "3:4" is 3 June.

One answer to the question of the date of Naomi's baptism might be that it occurred between 1 April and 15 April 1638, and that's the best that we can do. But the source provides a pattern that points to a more accurate and more satisfying resolution. The dates 1 April and 15 April are fourteen days apart, and reference to a perpetual calendar reveals that both of these dates were Sundays. Because most baptisms were celebrated on Sundays, there might have been several baptisms on any given Sunday. So we may conclude that the scribe who recorded these baptisms entered the date of baptism once, no matter how many children were baptized on a given day. In this case, the date 1 April 1638 covers the baptisms of both Ezekiel Fogg and Naomi Johnson.

Example Two: Discrepant Records

The earliest civil vital records for Boston, Massachusetts, state that "Elisabeth the daughter of Mr. John Winthrope the younger & Elisabeth his wife was born 24 (5) 1636 [24 July 1636]."[2] However, the Boston church records indicate that "Elizabeth the daughter of our brother John Winthrop the younger" was baptized at Boston on "the 3d of the 5th month 1636," that is, 3 July 1636.[3] Both these dates cannot be correct: Elizabeth cannot have been baptized before she was born.

In the case of discrepant records, it's important to cast about for another source of information. Fortunately with the Winthrop example, the great richness of the preserved Winthrop Papers permits an easy resolution of this discrepancy. On 3 July 1636, Adam Winthrop, then residing at Boston, wrote to his brother John Winthrop Jr., then residing at Saybrook, Connecticut, that "my sister is brought abed of a daughter thanks be to God and is well"[4] (Adam's "sister" was in fact his sister-in-law, the wife of John Jr.). And on 5 July 1636, Elizabeth (Fones) (Winthrop) Feake, widow of Henry Winthrop, also wrote to John Winthrop Jr., saying, "I rejoice with you and bless God for the safe delivery of my sister and the welfare of her and your daughter."[5] Thus, the church record is correct and the town record in error. Perhaps the town record merely has the wrong month, and the child was born on 24 June, but it may be wrong as to both the day and the month of the event.

Unfortunately, relatively few private sources such as the Winthrop Papers exist for this time period, so many other similar discrepancies between the Boston church and town records will not be resolved quite so easily. An alternative method available for these two sources is to subject them to source analysis. I underook this analysis as part of my Great Migration research, concluding that the early Boston church records are generally reliable, whereas the town vital records are not; when the two are in conflict, the church record will almost always be the preferred record.[6] Sometimes, then, record analysis will force you momentarily back to source analysis.

2. Who created the record?

This question—who created the record?—probes the reliability of the information contained in the record. Was the person who actually created the record good at his or her job? The creator might be a census enumerator, a minister, a tax collector, or a notary. It is unlikely that someone acting in a professional capacity would have direct knowledge of the event being recorded. Only by exploring a large number of records created by one of these officials can we judge their reliability, and so in such situations we revert to source analysis to answer this question.

Sometimes, of course, the creator of the record is also the provider of the information—which would give us an elevated degree of confidence in the reliability of the information. Sometimes it is possible to identify a will as holographic, meaning written by the testator rather than by a scribe or notary. The testator may state explicitly that he or she wrote the will, or it is clear that the signature matches the handwriting in the body of the will. Or perhaps, to take another record type, the minister is recording in his register the baptism of his own child.

When the creator of the record is *not* the same person as the provider of the information, the chance for an error in the transmission of accurate information increases, just as it does when the original of a document is being copied. The data may lose integrity through oral as well as written transmission.

3. Who provided the information?

The question of who provided the information is closely linked with the previous question, who created the record. It also probes the reliability of the information in the record. Did the person who provided the information to the creator of the record have *direct* knowledge of the event in question? Were there certain motivations that would cause him or her to exaggerate or alter the truth?

❯ Example One: Census Records

When the census enumerator appeared at the front door, who was home to answer the questions? In a small nuclear family, either the mother or the father would be expected to provide highly reliable answers to most of the questions. But what of a larger household, with in-laws, stepchildren, and servants? Most adults would be able to provide reliable information on the names and genders of all members of the household, but they might be hazy on ages and places of birth. If the husband was not at home, and the wife was that man's second wife, she would probably provide more accurate information about her own children than about the children her husband might have had with an earlier wife.

➤ Example Two: Nuncupative (Oral) Wills

An interesting situation arises with nuncupative wills (that is, oral wills). The record may have been created in two steps. First, the dying testator orally states his testamentary desires to the witnesses present. Then, at some later date, these witnesses relay this information to the scribe or court official, who puts it in writing. The chances for decay in the accuracy of the information are significantly increased. Do we know how reliable the witnesses were? Did they have any conflicting interests that might cause them to distort the wishes of the testator? How much time passed between the two events, between the oral statement of the testator and the writing of the record?

External Knowledge

Moving deeper into the analysis, we find that in order to determine the substance of what is in the records, and later to employ this substantive information in linking records together, we will need knowledge external to the sources and records themselves, both generic external knowledge and specific external knowledge.

Generic external knowledge consists of data and thought processes that are applicable across the board, regardless of the time and place you are researching. It might be something so simple and obvious as the rules of arithmetic and logic. Arithmetic comes into play when records provide you with a date and a person's age on that date, and you proceed to calculate a birth date on that basis. Simple logic assists when one record refers explicitly to another record, which is quite common; such cross-references allow you to link the two records with a very high degree of probability. Another form of generic external knowledge is provided by a perpetual calendar, which you might use to determine the day of the week on which some event took place. The normal human gestation period is another example of generic external knowledge used in genealogy: you would certainly doubt birthdates of siblings that are only a few months apart.

Specific external knowledge consists of information that might support genealogical reasoning and that varies from time to time and place to place. The commonest category of such knowledge relates to the laws and customs of a particular locality, such as the statutory consequences of intestate succession or the customary age at which a man or woman might marry. More will be said on this subject in Chapter Six.

Some of the knowledge that is useful for genealogical analysis does not fit so neatly into one or the other of these two categories. Until modern techniques of assisted reproduction came into being, there was a recognized range of childbearing years, say the early teens to the mid-forties, with exceptions known but rare. Within a given society, however, the acceptable date at which a woman might have her earliest child might differ from the biological norm. It is important to be aware of both biological and societal limits in performing analyses.

Case Studies

To delve more deeply into the topics discussed in this chapter, let's turn to some case studies: three specific records, relating to three different problems. (We will return to these three specific problems in later chapters as we work our way through the problem-solving sequence.) The goal is to subject these three records to the questions elaborated earlier, in an effort to extract from them the maximum of information on **substance** and **reliability.**

In the case of **substance**, we will be able to arrive at conclusions, sometimes tentative and sometimes firm, about such matters as the names of the principals participating in the recorded event, and perhaps their ages, residences, occupations, wealth, and other such matters.

In the case of **reliability**, we are generally gathering information that will allow us to make judgments at later stages in the analytic process. For example, we will decide who created the record and who provided the information, but we may need several records before we can determine the reliability of those creators and providers.

John Horne—Essex Quarter Courts *(cont. from Chapter One)*

Among the loose papers of the Essex County, Massachusetts, court are four depositions made by a man named John Horne (or some variant thereof), in which the deponent states his age. We will consider the first of these depositions here, and the remaining three in Chapter Three.

> Jno. Horne, aged about sixty years, deposed that he sold to Jno. Humphrieye, Esq., deceased, about one acre of land and a house where George Keisour has now built a tan house in Salem. Sworn 24: 1: 1661/2, before Wm. Hathorne[7]

This is an exact transcript of the abstract of the deposition as it appears in the published Essex County court records. Because the files themselves are currently inaccessible, we are hampered in addressing some of the questions we would like to have answered.

Assuming that this published abstract presents an accurate reflection of the content of the original deposition, there are some questions that we *can* answer.

When was the record created?

The date of the deposition is given as "24:1:1661/2," the 24th day of the first month of 1661/2. The double-dating for the year indicates that this court was using 25 March as the beginning of the calendar year. The first month was March, so we should interpret this date as 24 March 1661/2. (The next day according to the calendar then in use would have been 25 March 1662.)

Who created the record?

Did the deponent sign this document, and, if so, by mark or a full signature? If he did make a full signature, did he also write the body of the deposition himself, or is that in the hand of a court officer, presumably William Hathorne? As we are not at present able to examine the original of this deposition, this question must remain unanswered. In most cases, however, the depositions were written down by a court officer, in this case William Hathorne.

Who provided the information?

"Jno. Horne" was the deponent and therefore he provided the information.

What conclusions can we draw?

With the date of the deposition firmly in hand, we may subtract the stated age of the deponent, "about sixty years," from 24 March 1661/2 and calculate that "Jno. Horne" was born about 1602, perhaps late in 1601 or early in 1602 if we take the age at face value. Taken in isolation, a date stated in years ending in zero or five should be taken with some caution as possibly being rounded off and therefore more than one or two years off in one direction or another. (In this instance, we will alter our judgment on this point when we come to consider the remaining three depositions.)

Although the deponent does not state his residence as of 24 March 1661/2, we do learn that at some time in the past he owned land in Salem. Thus Salem may well have been, and may still be, his residence.

From this single record we have determined that "Jno. Horne" was born about 1602, that he was affluent enough to have owned land, and that he may have been a resident of Salem, Massachusetts.

John Borden— Middlesex Court Files

The loose papers of the Middlesex County, Massachusetts, court contain two records from the 1650s with the name John Borden or Bourden.

We will examine the first of these here; we will consider the second in Chapter Three, along with other records for a John Borden in Watertown. As reported in *The New England Historical and Genealogical Register* in 1849, citing Middlesex County Court Records,

> "John Bourden" appears in a list of men who took the Oath of Fidelity to Massachusetts Bay Colony in 1652.[8]

We are reliant here on the transcription of this list printed in the *Register* more than 150 years ago. The author of the article did not consult the original paper from the files, so another layer of copying has taken place, in or before 1849, in preparation for publication.

When was the record created?

The date of this record is 1652, with no month or day given.

Who created the record?

The list begins with six names not associated with any town; some can be identified as residents of Lancaster and Cambridge. There then follows the subheading "Watertown," after which forty-one names are listed, most recognizable as Watertown men. The Watertown section of the list may have been composed by a single town official, but the inclusion of men from other Middlesex towns suggests that the list as a whole was created by an unidentified county official. Therefore this list has probably been copied at least once, from the original individual town records, in 1652.

Who provided the information?

We have already concluded that the list as it exists probably was generated in two stages. That is, information was first supplied by town, from Lancaster, Cambridge, and Watertown, and then amalgamated into one list. Thus, there would also have been two levels of providers of this information. First, each individual choosing to take the Oath of Fidelity would have made his desires known to some town officer. Then, that town officer would have provided the town list to a county official. At the beginning of the creation of this list, then, we would have a process somewhat like a deposition, in which an individual is stating his name to a recorder.

What conclusions can we draw?

In 1652 in Massachusetts Bay, the Oath of Fidelity was administered to men aged sixteen and over. It did not carry with it the voting privileges associated with colony freemanship, so it does not imply prior admission to a Massachusetts Bay church. (These observations are examples of specific external knowledge.)

The first three names in the Watertown section of the list are Samuel Stratton Sr., Samuel Stratton Jr., and John Stratton, the first being father of the second and third. Samuel Jr. married in 1651 and John in 1659, so the birth years of the three men may be estimated as about 1600, 1626, and 1634 (based on the assumption that men at that time first married at about 25 years of age). This is not, then, just a list of young men not yet eligible for freemanship, but includes men of all ages.

In sum, since anyone included in this list must have been at least sixteen years old, we may conclude from this single record that a man named "John Bourden," born no later than 1636, but perhaps many years earlier, was residing in Watertown in 1652.

Rachel Hart—Winthrop Medical Journal *(cont. from Chapter One)*

The Winthrop Medical Journal contains five records for a patient named Rachel Hart. We will examine the first of these records here and the remaining four in Chapter Three.

> Hart Rachell of Farmington beginning to fall again into such vomiting as last year by which she lost her sight 2 doses 2 grains $ cum ebor sacc[aro][9] [the dollar sign is a crude approximation of one of the apothecary symbols employed by Winthrop]

This record has most of the formulaic elements that make up an entry in this source: surname; given name; residence; diagnosis; and treatment. Uncharacteristically, no age is given, and there is also no stated relationship to another person.

When was the record created?

This item appears in an early section of the journal, in a group of eight consecutive pages called "the loose sheets." These come after the earliest surviving pages of the journal, when Winthrop was residing at New Haven, and just before the major sequence of pages, organized by town, begun shortly after his move to Hartford.

Of the eight pages of the "loose sheets," the first three and the last three are dated at the top "Nov. 1657." The entry under discussion here is the third item on the fourth page, which does not have a year date, but has in the upper left corner "Nov. 21." Thus the date for this record would be 21 November 1657 (or perhaps a day or two later).

Who created the record?

In our earlier analysis of this source, we determined that all entries were made by John Winthrop Jr., and so he certainly created this entry.

Who provided the information?

Although John Winthrop Jr. occasionally practiced medicine at a distance, responding to descriptions of symptoms sent to him by letter, he saw most of his patients in person. He was residing at Hartford by late 1657, and Farmington was the town just to the west of Hartford. Winthrop may have made the short journey to Farmington to visit Rachel Hart and other patients, but it is more likely that Rachel traveled to Hartford to see Winthrop, and that the information in this entry came directly from her.

What conclusions can we draw?

First, as to substance, we learn that a woman named Rachel Hart was residing in Farmington, Connecticut, in late 1657, and she was suffering from vomiting that led to loss of her eyesight (a circumstance that will be of importance in interpreting other records). And this was not the first time she had been treated by Winthrop. The diagnosis in this entry is "beginning to fall again into such vomiting as last year by which she lost her sight," implying that he had treated Rachel sometime in 1656. (This is one of many entries that strongly indicate that John Winthrop Jr. had been acting as a physician long before the commencement of the surviving portions of the journal in 1657, and that some pages have been lost.)

Second, as to reliability, we have determined that John Winthrop Jr. created the record, based on information almost certainly supplied by the patient herself. Source analysis of Winthrop's Medical Journal showed that he was in general a careful and reliable reporter, but that on occasion he made minor errors of fact. This one record does not tell us much about the reliability of Rachel Hart, but we do know that Winthrop received his information directly from her (or perhaps from a close family member who accompanied her).

Summary

In this chapter we have described the second analytic tool, **record analysis**. We began with a definition: A **record** is that portion of a **source** which pertains to a single event.

After providing a few examples of record types, we proceeded, as in the previous chapter on source analysis, to probe some records with a range of questions, designed to elicit from the individual records the maximum amount of information on **substance** and **reliability**.

Although the list is not exhaustive, the questions posed to the records are:

- When was the record created?
- Who created the record?
- Who provided the information?

The case studies showed the variety of conclusions that might be extracted from a single record, conclusions that related to substance and reliability.

With the analytic tools of **source analysis** and **record analysis** now in hand, the next step is to explore the third analytic tool, **linkage analysis**, in which we will study the criteria for determining that two or more records pertain to the same individual.

Chapter Three

Linkage Analysis

This chapter is the hub about which the rest of the book turns, inasmuch as the linkage of records is the distinctive act of the genealogist, as stated in the Second Fundamental Rule: "You must have a sound, explicit reason for saying that any two individual records refer to the same person." Can you confirm with some reliability that this person in this particular record in this particular source is the same as another person in another record in another source? You will find applications for **linkage analysis** in most of the steps of the problem-solving sequence.

Some Definitions

In **linkage analysis**, you compare two or more **records**, or two or more **linkage bundles**, with a goal of determining whether or not they pertain to the same individual. As part of this process, you provide a **rationale** for your decisions.

> A **linkage bundle** is a collection of two or more **records** which, through the application of linkage analysis, you have determined to pertain to the same individual.

> A **dossier** is a collection of two or more **linkage bundles** which, through the application of linkage analysis, you have determined to pertain to the same individual.

> A **rationale** is a narrative that presents your arguments for creating a **linkage bundle**. The rationale implements the portion of the Second Fundamental Rule that asks that you have a "sound, explicit reason" for making your linkage decisions.

As you work through the solution of a genealogical problem, you will employ linkage analysis repeatedly, building structures of greater and greater complexity as you go. You will create hierarchies of linked records as you incorporate more and more of the evidence generated by and for an individual during his or her lifetime. Figure 3.1 is a graphic depiction of this process.

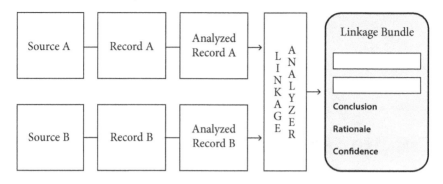

Figure 3.1. Linkage Analysis.

In this diagram, the two horizontal sequences (Source A — Record A — Analyzed Record A and Source B — Record B — Analyzed Record B) represent the work done by source analysis and record analysis, the third element in the First Fundamental Rule. The Linkage Analyzer represents your thought processes in deciding whether or not to join these two records together, implementing the Second Fundamental Rule. The Linkage Bundle records the results of this process and will be discussed in more detail below when we encounter an example of that construct.

A linkage bundle represents the lowest possible level of linkage analysis, in which you join together independent records to form an analytic construct. A dossier is the next step up in the hierarchy of proving a genealogical conclusion; you are no longer dealing with individual records, but with groups of records that have already been linked. This hierarchy can reach higher, with dossiers being linked to form yet more extensive dossiers, until you have gained your goal. *The solution of a genealogical problem is always the result of the joining of two or more linkage bundles or dossiers.*

A Toolkit for Linkage Analysis

In order to make linkage decisions, you need additional tools to assist in your analysis:

You will make linkage decisions based on the relative strength and reliability of **points of comparison**.

You will make your linkage decisions with various levels of confidence.

You will pay close attention to the analytic categories employed in making linkages.

Points of Comparison

The basic task of linkage analysis is to compare two records, two linkage bundles, or two dossiers, to determine the probability that any of these pairs of items pertain to the same person. In order to make this determination, the most important step is to identify in each pair as many points of comparison as possible. Linkage decisions are made on the basis of the number of points of comparison between any two items, and the relative strength and reliability of the various points of comparison.

Points of comparison comprise a wide range of identifying markers, including name, age, residence, occupation, and many others. Generally, no single marker, no single point of comparison will be sufficient for linking two items. In particular, two records that contain the same name should never be linked on that basis alone; "the name's the same" is never enough. One exception to that rule: when one record contains within it an explicit cross-reference to another record.

For some problems, just a few matching points of comparison will be sufficient for arriving at a robust and satisfactory conclusion, whereas in other instances a larger number of matching points of comparison will be necessary. For example, when you are dealing with a common surname, more points of comparison will be required than with a rarer surname.

Confidence Level of Conclusion

Genealogy is an empirical historical discipline, and as such conclusions are very rarely one hundred percent certain. They are never subject to mathematical proof. As you make each linkage decision, you must be alert to your level of confidence in those conclusions. Specifically:

Almost certain: As close to complete proof as you get, in excess of ninety percent. Similar to the legal standard of proof "beyond a reasonable doubt" as employed in criminal verdicts.

Highly probable: Well in excess of fifty percent, but not "almost certain."

Probable: More likely than not; barely fifty percent. Similar to the legal standard of proof by "preponderance of the evidence" as used in civil disputes.

Possible: Less than fifty percent, but not demonstrably impossible.

By the nature of genealogical reasoning, it is impossible to apply mathematical formulas by which to compute these probabilities. Rather, assign these confidence levels based on your developing experience as a genealogical analyst.

Because there is a subjective element in assigning probabilities, different genealogists will on occasion arrive at different estimates for these levels of probability. Don't let this discrepancy discourage you; such differences of opinion should stimulate further research and analysis.

Analytic Categories

The analytic categories employed when making linkage decisions are the following:

Source analysis
Record analysis
Linkage analysis
Generic external knowledge
Specific external knowledge

In working through the case studies, we will indicate when we are applying these categories.

Steps in Linkage Analysis

The usual sequence of steps undertaken in the task of linking together two or more records with the goal of building up a coherent picture of some individual is as follows:

1. *Select records:* Select two or more records, usually on the basis that a certain name of interest occurs in each. These records may be from a single source or from several sources, from one locality or several, from a narrow time or from a range of decades. Except in the simplest of problems, where there are very few records to begin with, you should begin with a small set of records, perhaps from one locality, as you build your first linkage bundles, on the path to a complete portrayal of a person of interest.

2. *Examine points of comparison:* Look for pieces of evidence in each record that allow you to deduce that two records refer to one person, or, alternatively, that two records pertain to two separate persons. In some instances, you will not be able to decide one way or another.

3. *Analyze discrepancies:* In assessing whether two records may be linked, investigate discrepancies in the evidence to determine whether some potential error in the records is pointing you in the wrong direction.

4. *Make linkage decision and draw conclusions:* Once you are comfortable in declaring that two or more records (or dossiers) pertain to the same person, state that decision. Then, determine whether any other facts about that person may be inferred from the linked records which could not be derived from any of the records taken in isolation.

5. *Construct rationale:* Generate the narrative justifying the linkage decisions and inferences made in the previous step.

6. *Estimate confidence level:* Finally, before moving on to the next group of selected records, and the next series of linkage decisions, assess the probability of the accuracy of the conclusions you have just reached. Are the linkages almost certain, highly probable, probable, or merely possible?

As we work through the case studies and examples in the remainder of the book, we will illustrate the linkage analysis process with diagrams of linkage bundles and dossiers. The last three steps listed above correspond to the three main elements in the body of the diagrams: Conclusion; Rationale; Confidence.

Some Simple Linkage Bundles

We will work through a series of progressively more complicated examples to demonstrate linkage analysis (also called **record linkage**), beginning with the simplest of linkage events, in which we connect two elements within the same record to derive a new result. Next will be the linkage of two records of the same type. Finally, we will examine three case studies in which multiple records are linked; in two of these examples the records will be from the same source and of the same type, while in the third example the records will be of different types from different sources. All of these examples illustrate the lowest level of linkage analysis, in which two or more records are tied together to create a linkage bundle. We will examine higher levels of analysis, the creation of dossiers and, finally, problem resolution, in later chapters.

Linkage Within a Single Record

One might think naively that in order to perform record linkage, at least two distinct records are needed. Remarkably, however, record linkage can take place within a single record. On 7 November 1678, "John Edy of Watertowne in the Coun[ty] of Midd[lesex] in New England yeom[an]" sold a parcel of land in Watertown to "Thomas Streayte of the same town plant[e]r." When the grantor signed the deed, he did so as "Jno. Eddy Sen[io]r."[1]

The juxtaposition of both the description of the grantor and a separate signature for the grantor permit us to make the linkage. This signature tells us first that there was more than one John Eddy in Watertown, and that the grantor of this deed was the eldest of these (without implying anything about the genealogical relationships among the various John Eddys). The linkage event occurs when we notice that the grantor is also referred to in the same record as "yeoman," thus providing us with the occupation of the eldest John Eddy in Watertown in 1678. This sort of linkage is a close cousin of the case where we have within one record an explicit cross-reference to another record. This knowledge will be of great utility in sorting out the various John Eddys in Watertown as we study more records for these men.

(We could make the argument that there are actually two records in this example. The body of the deed, which contains the first version of the grantor's name, was probably created by a scribe or clerk, while the grantor himself would have added his signature, perhaps at a different time. Under such an interpretation, the later acknowledgement of the deed by the grantor, and then the recording of the deed, could also be seen as separate records, since they would have occurred on different dates, and so would have been separate events, potentially with additional consequences for our analysis.)

Assuming that the record analysis of this deed has not revealed any potential defects in this record, there can be little doubt that the eldest John Eddy in Watertown in 1678 was a yeoman. In this particular circumstance of linkage within a single record, we have reached the confidence level of "almost certain." (See Figure 3.2.)

Linkage Bundle: John Eddy

"John Edy of Watertowne…, yeoman," 7 November 1678

"Jno. Eddy Sen[io]r," 7 November 1678

Conclusion: On 7 November 1678, there was more than one man named John Eddy in Watertown, Massachusetts. The grantor of this deed was the oldest of these men named John Eddy and his occupation was yeoman.

Rationale: These two records occur in the same document, the first in the body of the deed and the second as the signature appended to that deed. Although these two pieces of the deed may have been made at separate times, by the very nature of a deed they pertain to the same person, thus telling us that the man designated Senior on this date was a yeoman. The conclusion that he was the eldest of that name in Watertown on that date is based on the accepted usage of the terms Senior and Junior in early New England.

Confidence: Almost certain.

Figure 3.2.

The figure just above is a diagrammatic depiction of the results and some of the process of creating a linkage bundle, and will be employed repeatedly hereafter. The unshaded rectangles contain the evidence, the analyzed but unlinked records. The shaded area encapsulates the evidence, and presents the conclusions derived from that evidence, the rationale for reaching those conclusions, and the confidence level of the conclusions. As we shall see, these linkage bundles can themselves be linked together and embedded in higher level constructs known as dossiers, which will be represented by diagrams of their own.

Linkage of Two Records

Richard Wright arrived in New England in 1630 and over the next four decades lived a peripatetic existence, residing at Lynn, Boston, Braintree, Rehoboth, and Ipswich, Massachusetts, and Twelve Mile Island, and Podunk, Connecticut.[2] Wright certainly resided briefly in Boston very shortly after his arrival in New England, for he was admitted to Boston church as member #89, which would have been in late 1630.[3] The various genealogists who have studied Richard Wright also place him in Boston in the 1660s, based on two deeds:[4]

On 21 December 1660, Edward Rawson conveyed to Thomas Danforth, Edmond Batter, and Samuel Torrey, as feoffees in trust for Rawson's wife, "all that his dwelling house . . . and two acres of garden & pasture thereto adjoining situate and being in Boston & bounded by the street east and the common west, the lands of Ephraim Pope & Anthony Stoddard south, the lands of Xtopher [Christopher] Batt, John Blower, **Richard Wright,** Richard Cooke, Tho[mas] Clarke & William Pollard north."[5]

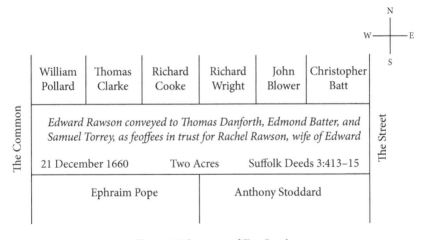

Figure 3.3. Summary of First Deed.

On 25 October 1670, Edward Rawson and Rachel his wife sold to John Pynchon "all that his mansion or dwelling house situate, lying & being in Boston with the outhousing [and] gardens fenced in before the said dwelling house to a three foot of the stile going over the lane which the said Edward Rawson hath made dividing his land with all the land within that fence up the said lane to the common being near one acre, . . . bounded by the street to Roxbury on the east, the lane on the south, the common on the west, the lands of William Pollard, Thomas Clarke, Richard Cooke, **Richard Wright,** John Blower & Ann & Thomas Batt on the north."[6]

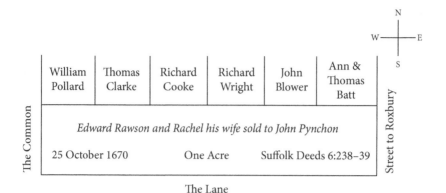

Figure 3.4. Summary of Second Deed.

These two records present a common situation—one in which the problem changes from attempting to link two individuals to attempting to link two pieces of land. When we compare the two deeds (see Figures 3.3 and 3.4), we see that two of the four boundaries are the same: the common to the west and the street to the east. In the second deed, Edward Rawson is kind enough to inform us that he has, sometime in the 1660s, divided the earlier two-acre lot into two one-acre lots, by running a lane through the lot from east to west. Thus, the south bound, which was formerly the land of Ephraim Pope and Anthony Stoddard, is now the newly constructed lane.

This leaves us with the north boundary. Note that, with one exception, the names listed in the two deeds for the north bound are the same, but with the order of names in the second deed reversed. The one exception is that Christopher Batt in the 1660 deed has been replaced by Ann and Thomas Batt in the second deed. Christopher Batt died at Boston on 10 August 1661; Ann Batt was his wife and Thomas Batt his eldest son. As a result, we may state with a high degree of certainty that the north bounds in these two deeds match. The likelihood that these same six individuals would be in possession of six parcels, in the same sequence, in two different locations in Boston is exceedingly small.

Having determined that the parcels of land conveyed in these two deeds were identical, the next step is to turn the focus of the investigation back to the identity of the men named Richard Wright in the two deeds. We may say with high probability that these two records identify one Richard Wright, who held a lot in

Boston at least from 1660 to 1670. That completes linkage analysis for these two deeds. (See Figure 3.5.)

Linkage Bundle: Richard Wright

On 21 December 1660, Edward Rawson placed in trust a parcel of land in Boston, the northern abutters of which were Christopher Batt, John Blower, Richard Wright, Richard Cooke, Thomas Clarke and William Pollard

On 25 October 1670, Edward Rawson and Rachel his wife sold to John Pynchon a parcel of land in Boston, the northern abutters of which were William Pollard, Thomas Clarke, Richard Cooke, Richard Wright, John Blower and Ann and Thomas Batt

Conclusion: These two deeds refer to the same parcel of land.

Rationale: Two observations are needed to make the two lists of northern abutters coincide. First, Ann and Thomas Batt of the second deed are widow and son of Christopher Batt of the second deed, and administrators of his estate. Second, with this conclusion in hand, we note that the sequence of abutters in the second deed is identical with that in the first deed, but reversed. Although not included in the extracts given above, the eastern and western boundaries of the two deeds are the same, and the second deed provides internally an explanation for the difference in the description of the southern boundary. The probability that two parcels of land in early Boston could share so many points of comparison in their boundaries without being identical is very low. (Further research on other land records involving these same abutters could further decrease this probability.)

Confidence: Almost certain.

Figure 3.5.

At this point, we have achieved the main goal of this example: demonstrating how to link two similar records. However, if we take a moment to follow this problem a bit further, we arrive at an unexpected and interesting result. Our focus on the two deeds arose as a very small part of the story of the immigrant Richard Wright. Having connected the two deeds, thus showing a segment of the history of a parcel of land in Boston, we would naturally want to discover how Richard Wright obtained this land.

Several additional deeds for land in Boston show further variants of the string of six parcels that form the northern boundary of the parcel transferred in the two deeds above. (These six parcels were the house lots on the south side of what is now School Street, one of the earliest-settled parts of Boston.) Surprisingly, none of these additional deeds names Richard Wright, but many of them do name a *Robert* Wright.

For example, on 8 June 1652, William Aspinwall sold to "my son-in-law John Angier my dwelling house in Boston, together with my garden, orchard & close containing two acres or thereabouts being bounded on the north with the lots of Thomas Woodward, [blank] Barker, Richard Cooke, Robert Wright & Thomas Bomsteed & Thomas Grubb, on the east with the high street, Ephraim Pope & Mr. Anthony Stoddard on the south & the common on the west."[7] The east, south, and west bounds of this deed are the same as those of the first of the Edward Rawson deeds presented above. The string of six parcels on the north side is also there, but with an almost complete change of ownership in each of the lots between 1652 and 1660. Another deed, dated 20 May 1684, also includes as abutters these same six parcels, and in this list we find "Robert Right Sr." [8]

The dates of these two deeds naming Robert Wright bracket the dates of the deeds naming Richard Wright as the owner of this parcel. In addition, there are other Boston records for a man named Robert Wright during this time period. (We might hypothesize that the appearances of Richard Wright as holder of the parcel in 1660 and 1672 indicated that Richard was son of Robert and had inherited the land, as was the case for the nearby parcel held by the Batt family. But such a hypothesis conflicts with the evidence of the 1684 deed showing this parcel still held by Robert Wright. The Richard Wright who arrived in 1630 was born about 1596. His father would have been born no later than the early 1570s, and so would not have been alive in 1684; thus we reject the possibility that Robert was father of Richard.)

We conclude that the two Boston deeds that initially attracted our attention, ostensibly for the much-traveled Richard Wright, should actually be linked to another man, Robert Wright of Boston. We may postulate that in the 1660 deed a simple clerical error was made, and that this deed was used in the preparation of the 1670 deed and the error was replicated. Although Richard Wright had resided briefly in Boston in the 1630s, there is no evidence that he returned there in the 1660s, and so one entry may be removed from his list of migrations within New England.

Case Studies: Some More Complicated Linkage Bundles

John Horne (cont. from Chapter Two)

In Chapter Two we analyzed a single record for a man named John Horne. As it happens, many records containing this name are found in Salem town records, Essex County records, and Massachusetts Bay Colony records. The discussion here is limited to four records only.

These records are found in the published Essex County Quarterly Court records:[9]

"Jno. Horne" deposed "aged about sixty years" on 24 March 1661/2

"Deacon Horn" deposed "aged seventy-two years" in June 1674

"Jno. Horne, Sr.," deposed "aged about seventy-four years" in July 1675

"John Horne" deposed "aged about eighty-one years" on 28 February 1683/4

We have already discussed the Essex Quarterly Court records in Chapter One, Source Analysis (see page 19), and have also dissected the first of these four records in Chapter Two, Record Analysis (see page 28). For the purposes of this discussion, we will assume that all four of these items have been subjected to proper and complete record analysis, and that all four as published are accurate abstracts of the surviving contemporary depositions.

Our source and record analyses have shown that not only are these four records all from the same source, but they are all of the same form; all are depositions made orally and recorded by a court clerk. Each, therefore, represents direct testimony by the deponent about his age on a given date.

Although the depositions provide much more information, some about the deponent himself and more about others involved in the case in contention (different in each of the four records), for the moment we are concerned with only three points of comparison from each deposition: name of deponent, age of deponent, and date of deposition.

Name of Deponent

Let's now take up each of these markers. In the four records the name appears in four different forms. Four elements of the name are in play: spelling of the given name; spelling of the surname; title of "Deacon"; and designation as "Sr." The first two of these are trivial: "Jno." was an abbreviation for John at that time, and the spelling of surnames had not become stabilized by the end of the seventeenth century. Still, they can be stumbling blocks for genealogists who are unfamiliar with the customs of a given time and place. And in other circumstances these issues could be more problematic.

The question of the office of deacon is resolved by a separate act of record linkage. The deposition of June 1674 is one of two which have been preserved in the proceedings against Doctor George Emery for drunkenness, the other deposition being given by John Guppy. In the record of this court action, the court ordered the accused to "pay witnesses, John

Horne, Sr., John Guppy and Peeter Harvey."[10] This linkage of two records is relatively straightforward, as it depends solely on the court's practices and recordkeeping procedures, and not on anything intrinsic to the individuals involved. Thus, in June 1674, "John Horne Sr." was also "Deacon Horne." Figure 3.6 is a diagram of this linkage bundle.

Linkage Bundle: John Horne no. 1

On 25 May 1674, "Deacon Horn, aged seventy-two years," deposed that "he see Doctor Emery fall to the ground twice and sayeth that he did verily believe him to be in drink." (This was followed by a similar deposition by John Guppy.)

On 30 June 1674, "Mr. George Emory forfeited his bond for appearance in his presentment for excessive drinking and was ordered to pay witnesses, John Horne Sr., John Guppy and Peeter Harvey."

Conclusion: In mid-1674, John Horne Senior was deacon of his church.

Rationale: By its dating and placement in the court records, the 25 May 1674 deposition apparently pertains to the 30 June 1674 court case. This conclusion is strengthened by the match between the two depositions actually given by Horne and Guppy, and the list of witnesses to be paid: Horne, Guppy, and Harvey. The Harvey deposition has seemingly not survived. Thus, the Deacon Horne of 25 May is the same man as the John Horne Sr. of 30 June.

Confidence: Almost certain.

Figure 3.6.

The conclusion that "John Horne, Sr.," was also "Deacon Horne" is reinforced in a similar manner in the fourth record above: a 28 February 1683/4 deposition by "John Horne" in the case of Mr. Daniel Davison v. George Car[r], in which several other deponents refer to him as "Deacon Horne."[11]

Finally, let's consider the appellation of "Sr.," which at this time in New England simply designated the eldest of two or more men in town with the same name. It implies nothing about kinship. Senior might be older than Junior by one day, and be totally unrelated, or he might be older by decades and even be the grandfather of Junior. Resolving whether John Horne Sr. is the same as the John Horne in the other records depends on a full-scale investigation of all men named John Horne during the decades of interest. It is possible, for example, that the John Horne Sr. who was deacon in 1674 died not long after, and that by 1684 a younger man of the same name, but younger by only a few months, had succeeded both to the office and to the top of the seniority ladder. In our example, however, further analysis does not support this more complicated scenario.

Based solely on analysis of the different forms of the name in these four records, we can conclude that all refer to a man named John Horne, and that nothing precludes them all from referring to the same individual.

Age of Deponent and Date of Deposition

Moving along to age of deponent, we look at the calculated birthdates for John Horne based on the four records: 1602, 1602, 1601, and 1603. The consistency in the dates leads to a high probability that all four records pertain to the same individual. For four depositions given over the span of more than two decades, the statements of age are remarkably consistent, assuming they all pertain to the same individual.

Usually when someone's age is rounded to the nearest ten, as in the first record's "about sixty years," it is assumed that the age may be off by as much as five years. In this example, however, the four ages are so close that we can conclude that "about sixty years" is just as accurate as the other three ages. Thus we can conclude that John Horne Sr. was a very careful and accurate reporter, which should help when we encounter other records that he may have generated. We have, in fact, performed a bit of record analysis in the midst of our linkage analysis, answering the question "How reliable is this witness?" and thus demonstrating again the dialectical nature of the problem-solving process.

In sum, in the process of linking these four records, we have learned that there was one man by the name of John Horne in Salem from 1661 to 1684 who could claim the rank of "Senior," that he was born about 1602 (give or take a year, but no more), that he was for most of that period a deacon in the Salem church, and that he was a man who reported carefully and accurately. Figure 3.7 diagrams this additional linkage bundle for John Horne.

This is a substantial haul of information from four slender items. We relied on four analytic categories to reach these conclusions:

- Record analysis: Selection of four records of same type, that is, depositions that represent direct testimony by the deponent
- Linkage analysis: recourse to separate record linkage for the connection of "Deacon Horne" to "John Horne Sr."; and recourse to several separate record linkages for resolution of "Senior" vs. "Junior" status
- Generic external knowledge: Calculation of year of birth from date of deposition and age stated in deposition
- Specific external knowledge: the use of "Jno." as an abbreviation for "John" in colonial New England; the use of the terms "Sr." and "Jr." in colonial New England; and spelling variations of surnames in colonial New England

Linkage Bundle: John Horne no. 2

On 24 March 1661/2, "Jno. Horne" deposed that he was "aged about sixty years."

On 25 May 1674, "Deacon Horn deposed that he was "aged seventy-two years."

On 20 July 1675, "Jno. Horne Sr." deposed that he was "aged about seventy-four years."

On 28 February 1683/4, "John Horne" deposed that he was "aged about eighty-one years."

Conclusion: From 1661 to 1684, there was one man in Salem named John Horne who could, at least toward the end of that time, claim the rank of "Senior." He was born about 1602 and was deacon in the Salem church. He was a careful and accurate reporter of facts.

Rationale: An earlier linkage bundle demonstrated that "Deacon Horn" of the second of these records was John Horne. The ages given in these four depositions are highly consistent; the birth years calculated from them fall into a very narrow time frame. For us to believe that these four records pertained to more than one man by the name of John Horne, we would have to believe that there were two John Hornes of almost exactly the same age. Additional records for the name John Horne would either strengthen or disprove our conclusion. Having decided that these four records pertain to the same man, the conclusions regarding his age rank, his church office, and his reporting ability follow easily.

Confidence: Highly probable.

Figure 3.7.

Rachel Hart *(cont. from Chapter Two)*

Let's return now to Rachel Hart of the Winthrop Medical Journal (see page 31). Including the record for Rachel Hart examined in Chapter Two, five instances of this name are found in the same source.[12]

> 21 November 1657: Hart Rachell of Farmingto[n] beginning to fall again into such vomiting as last year [one word illegible] she lost her sight

> 1 February 1657/8: Hart Rachell 16 years lost her sight by vomiting naturally . . .

> 29 March 1658: Hart Rachell page 23 . . .

> 1 June 1658: Hart Rachell page 36 . . .

> 18 March 1658/9: Hart Rachell page 51

Points of Comparison

The first two of these records, separated by less than three months, share two points of comparison: the same name and the same diagnosis. Identity of name alone is never enough to justify the linkage of two records, but the identity of the diagnosis provides an additional shared marker that greatly increases the probability that the two Rachel Harts are the same.

Proceeding provisionally on the assumption that this linkage is correct, the second entry provides an additional piece of information that adds to our knowledge of Rachel Hart. Her age is given as sixteen on 1 February 1657/8, placing her birth in 1642 or thereabouts.

At this early stage of the creation of a linkage bundle for a Rachel Hart, we can see that linkage analysis is a synergistic process that provides increasing knowledge as more and more records are conjoined. Based on just two linked records, we can state that Rachel Hart who was born about 1642 was in late 1657 and early 1658 residing in Farmington, Connecticut. The conjunction of the name, the age, and the place of residence arises from the joining of the two records, and is not found in any one of the unlinked records.

Internal Cross-references

The third, fourth, and fifth entries share yet another feature that very strongly ties these entries to the second. Each of these records includes a back-reference to an earlier page on which the same name appears; these entries lack a diagnosis or statement of the patient's malady, and these back-references serve as a substitute for that portion of the standard entry. Such internal cross-references, when they are available, provide some of the strongest evidence for linking records, and allow us to reach conclusions with very high levels of confidence.

In order to exploit these internal cross-references, we must revert to source analysis momentarily, by exploring how Winthrop numbered the pages of his own source. The 29 March 1658 entry refers to "page 23," but since the Winthrop Medical Journal comprises loose sheets of paper as well as several gatherings of various numbers of sheets, Winthrop's own page numbers do not match the modern pagination now used for citation. (The citations in note 12 refer to the modern page numbers.) Thus we must be sure to check Winthrop's own page numbers when checking the cross-references. Looking at the entry for 1 February 1657/8, we see that it appears on page 23 of what Winthrop designated the Hartford section of his notes; thus the third record clearly refers to the second. Similarly, when checking Winthrop's back-references for the fourth and fifth entries against his own original pagination, we again find that they match. Assuming that we find Winthrop a convincing witness (and we do), this internal evidence links these last four entries together about as tightly as possible for historical records.

Finally, when we tie this conclusion together with our earlier provisional judgment that the first and second entries pertain to the same individual, we find that we have created a linkage bundle, in which five records from one source document about a year and a half in the life of a single person, Rachel Hart of Farmington, born about 1642. (See Figure 3.8.)

In the second, third, and fourth of these five entries, Winthrop recorded a number of follow-on treatments over the course of a few months, indicating that his attention to this patient was almost continuous for more than a year. The fifth entry, after the fragment given here, is blank, and no further information is found in this source for a woman of this name.

Linkage Bundle: Rachel Hart no. 1

21 November 1657: Hart Rachell of Farmington beginning to fall again into such vomiting . . . she lost her sight.

1 February 1657/8: Hart Rachell 16 years lost her sight by vomiting.

29 March 1658: Hart Rachell page 23 . . .

1 June 1658: Hart Rachell page 36 . . .

18 March 1658/9: Hart Rachell page 51 . . .

Conclusion: These five records pertain to one woman named Rachel Hart, born about 1642 and, at least at the time of the first record, residing at Farmington. She suffered from problems with her eyesight.

Rationale: We can conclude that the first two records refer to the same person because both were suffering from the same disease. The last three records are linked firmly to the second record by the chain of back references to the appropriate page in the medical journal. (The page citations are the modern archival page numbers; the original page numbers given by Winthrop also appear on most pages and allow the cross-references to be confirmed.) The estimated year of birth derives from the age given in the second record and the date of that record.

Confidence: Almost certain.

Figure 3.8.

Additionally, not all **data collection** will be the result of a carefully planned campaign of research (see Chapter 6 for more information on data collection). We must always be open to the opportunities provided by serendipity. Referring again to the first of the entries for Rachel Hart, dated 21 November 1657, we observe that the next entry is for another member of the same family.

> 21 November 1657: Hart Steven her brother great cough Φ cum saccaro to mix with honey & to take with honey & butter[13]

We will return to this record, and to this problem as a whole, in Chapter Seven (see page 101).

John Borden *(cont. from Chapter Two)*

Another set of four records, but of a slightly more complicated nature, was generated in Watertown, Massachusetts, in the space of six years:[14]

> "John Bourden" appears in a list of Watertown men who took the Oath of Fidelity to Massachusetts Bay Colony, 1652

> "Jo Borden" was owed 9s. by the town of Watertown, 22 October 1653

> "John Borden" was paid 9s. in January 1654/5, pursuant to "the [Watertown] Town Rate in the hands of Thomas Underwood which was granted in October 1653"

> "John Borden" was called "my late apprentice" by Charles Chadwick of Watertown, 20 February 1657[/8?]

In contrast to the case of John Horne, this set of records is more heterogeneous. The first is a colony record, the second and third are town records, and the fourth is a deposition entered in Middlesex County Court. None of the records represent the direct testimony of the person we are interested in.

Another difference from the Horne example is that these are the only known records for a man of this name in Watertown at any time in the seventeenth century. If we conclude that these four records pertain to the same individual, we do not have the potential concern of separating out two or more men of the same name over a period of several decades. On the assumption that all four of these records are for one person, it would seem that John Borden had only a brief residence in Watertown.

Internal Cross-references

Let's begin by following the line of least resistance, looking at the third record, which contains an explicit reference to the second. A list of debts owed by the town was drawn up in October 1653, and, more than a year later, the town ordered that those debts be discharged. So the second and third records clearly pertain to the same man.

Name

Like "Jno.," "Jo" was a common abbreviation for "John." In fact, this abbreviation is frequently used in the Watertown records, always representing John (never Joseph or Jonathan or anything else). "Bourden" is a perfectly ordinary variant of "Borden"; the slightly different spelling in no way prevents the first record from pertaining to the same man as the other three.

Age

Nothing in the second and third records indicates anything precise about the age of John Borden (except perhaps that he was not a child). We have already seen the first of these records in the chapter on record analysis (see pages 29–31), where we extracted some limited information on age. As noted previously, the Oath of Fidelity was taken by males aged 16 and older, so this John Borden would have been born no later than 1636. An apprenticeship would normally begin in the mid-teens and end in the early twenties, covering a period of about seven years. All of these parameters are subject to variation, but if Charles Chadwick had released John Borden just before the date of his deposition, then we might estimate that Borden was born about 1637, give or take a year or two.

The first and fourth records, then, are very much consistent with one another. We do not know what civic service John Borden performed to earn his nine shillings, but an apprentice might have done a number of things, such as bringing in a fox head for the bounty. The consistency of these four records, combined with the lack of any other Watertown records for this name, leads to reasonable confidence that they all do pertain to the same John Borden.

The resulting picture is that of a young man in his mid-teens at the time when these records were created, born about 1637, coming into town in 1652 or slightly earlier to serve his apprenticeship, and then leaving town late in 1657 or early in 1658, soon after completing his service. Figure 3.9 shows a linkage bundle for John Borden.

Thus, the analytical categories used to reach these conclusions include:

- Specific external knowledge: the understanding that the abbreviation "Jo" in colonial New England (and particularly in Watertown) stood for "John"; the variation in surname spelling in colonial New England; the minimum age for Oath of Fidelity in Massachusetts Bay in 1652

Linkage Bundle: John Borden no. 1

"John Bourden" appears in a list of Watertown men who took the Oath of Fidelity to Massachusetts Bay Colony, 1652.

"Jo Borden" was owed 9s. by the town of Watertown, 22 October 1653.

"John Borden" was paid 9s. in January 1654/5, pursuant to the [Watertown] Town Rate in the hands of Thomas Underwood which was granted in October 1653."

"John Borden" was called "my late apprentice" by Charles Chadwick of Watertown, 20 February 1657[/8?].

Conclusion: These four records pertain to one man named John Borden, residing at Watertown from 1652 to 1658. He was probably born about 1637, give or take a year or two.

Rationale: The differences in spelling are within the normal range of variance of the time, and so all four records refer to a John Borden. The second and third of these records may be linked with one another since the third states that it is the payment of the town debt mentioned in the second.

The Oath of Fidelity was administered to men between the ages of 16 and 60, so the John Borden of the first record was born no later than about 1636. If the John Borden of the fourth record had just completed his apprenticeship, and had been apprenticed at the usual age, he would have been about 21 in 1658, and so born about 1637.

All these records are consistent with one another if we assume that they pertain to the same person, and they are the only records for a man named John Borden in Watertown during these years.

Confidence: Highly probable.

Figure 3.9.

was at least 16; and knowledge pertaining to apprenticeship practices in early New England

- Generic external knowledge: pointer in one record to another

- Linkage analysis: in the negative sense that there are no other records available to link, which, combined with the high **record density,** increases the probability that the records under consideration refer to the same individual (see Chapter Six for more information on record density)

Summary

In demonstrating the process of linkage analysis, we have set forth three definitions, three tools for analysis, and a six-step process for making linkage decisions. Following this apparatus, we worked through a number of case studies, augmented by linkage bundle diagrams which illustrate the full implementation of the Second Fundamental Rule.

The three terms defined are

- Linkage bundle
- Dossier
- Rationale

The analytic toolkit comprises three items

- Points of comparison
- Confidence level of conclusion
- Analytic categories

The six steps of linkage analysis are

- Select records
- Examine points of comparison
- Analyse discrepancies
- Make linkage decision and draw conclusions
- Construct rationale
- Estimate level of confidence

In this chapter, we have applied record linkage at the lowest level, connecting just a handful of records with one another, leading to the creation of a **linkage bundle**. The creation of a single small linkage bundle will almost never be enough to solve a genealogical problem. In later chapters we will extend our linkage efforts, by connecting two or more linkage bundles with one another, and moving on to even higher levels of linkage in our search for solutions.

Having explored the analytic tools of source analysis, record analysis, and linkage analysis, we now turn to the steps involved in solving a genealogical problem, which is the focus of Part Two.

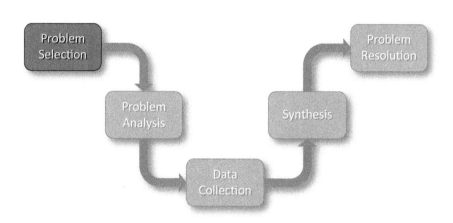

Chapter Four

Problem Selection

For most genealogists, the selection of a problem for research is an automatic process and may seem too trivial to deserve a chapter of its own. You might, for example, be aware of the name of a great-grandfather and ask yourself, without further reflection, who his parents were. Having asked this question, you are naturally inclined to decide immediately which types of records to investigate. But let's stop for a few moments and examine more closely the process of selecting a problem. In doing so, we will have the opportunity to examine some basic genealogical concepts that are important at all stages of research. Also, by disciplining yourself to think carefully of this first step in the research process, you will further the development of more orderly thought processes for all genealogical work you may undertake.

Ideally there "exists" a total and ideal genealogical network: the complete and accurate depiction of the biological relationships of all persons who have ever lived. The goal of all genealogical work is to approach this ideal network as closely as possible. But there are many reasons why the work of genealogical mortals falls short, and will always fall short, of this ideal. Records do not exist in many times and places, or, if they do exist, they are too fragmentary or indefinite to allow reconstruction of biological relationships. In cases where records do permit reconstruction of kinship networks, there may be undiscoverable discrepancies between the biological relationships and the historical or legal relationships. In the days before modern adoption procedures took effect, for example, children may have been informally taken into families, making them indistinguishable from the biological children of that set of parents. In other cases, there may be doubts as to the paternity of a child, and these non-paternity events may not even be known to the parties directly involved.

As genealogists, then, we hope to approach as close to the ideal network as possible, but we should always be aware that we will never achieve this goal. As a consequence, at any stage of the work, we must deal with the partial and fragmentary kinship networks that existing records provide. The attempt to link two or more previously unconnected partial networks is the core and essence of all genealogical work. In the remainder of the book we'll explore ways to weld partial networks to one another.

The Concept of "Genealogically Defined"

One of the most important concepts in this system of genealogical analysis is that of a person being **genealogically defined**.

> Any person is **genealogically defined** if we have at least one piece of evidence that will lead to the identification of his or her parents, one piece of evidence for each spouse, and one piece of evidence for each child.

At the very beginning of any genealogical inquiry, there is great value in drawing diagrams of the problem to be solved. The generic diagram shown here (Figure 4.1) demonstrates the meaning and implications of **genealogically defined**.

Focus on John Smith in the center of the chart. The dotted box drawn around him intersects a number of lines on the chart that connect him to other individuals. The dotted box crosses the line connecting John Smith to his parents, the line connecting him to his spouse (in this instance only one wife), and the line connecting him and his wife to their children. This set of connections fully defines John Smith

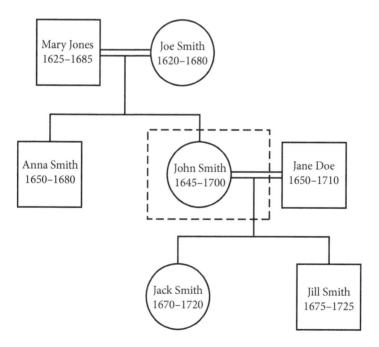

Figure 4.1. John Smith, "genealogically defined."

genealogically. Much more biographical information about John Smith may be discoverable, but nothing more genealogical.

You can trace any degree of relationship on a pedigree chart by shifting the dotted box from person to person and reading off the kinship relation designated by each connecting line.

For a person to be genealogically defined, you need at least one record that provides some information about each individual at the other end of the connecting lines intersected by the dotted box. In the case of John Smith, all you need to complete that portion of his genealogical definition pertaining to his wife is one record to indicate that he had a wife; in fact, you do not even have to have a given name for that wife. For example, a burial record might say that "the wife of John Smith" was buried on such and such a date. That record would be enough to satisfy the spousal portion of the genealogical definition of John Smith. The focus of your research could then shift to this unnamed wife of John Smith, and you would attempt to render her genealogically defined.

In brief, one verified, reliable, contemporary record is necessary and sufficient (a) to establish the existence of an individual, (b) to justify placing that individual on a pedigree chart, and (c) to complete one element in the genealogical definition of an immediately adjacent individual on the same chart.

Case Studies

Anna Dewey

Let's look next at the diagram of a single, moderately complicated family network (Figure 4.2). Near the center of the diagram is Anna Dewey (1643–1707). She is connected by an ascending line to Thomas Dewey and Frances (_____) Clark, her parents. She is connected by two parallel horizontal lines to John Woodward, her only husband, and by descending lines to two sons (Henry Woodward and John Woodward) and to one daughter (Elizabeth Woodward). (Other children are known, but we have omitted them here because of space considerations.) What more can we know about this woman genealogically? The answer is nothing.

Put more concretely, if we were to draw a dotted box around this Anna Dewey on the chart, it would intersect only the ascending, descending, and horizontal parallel lines. Applying this same process to the rest of the chart, only three people are completely genealogically defined: Anna Dewey, her husband John Woodward, and John Woodward's sister Freedom Woodward (assuming all her children have been identified). If the reasoning behind this chart is correct, there is no need or possibility for more genealogical work on these individuals, and we must look elsewhere if we are to find a genealogical problem upon which to focus our efforts. (However, to say that a person is "genealogically defined" does not mean that research on that person is complete. It may be possible to find much additional biographical information, but this does not come within the narrow definition of "genealogically defined" in use in this book.)

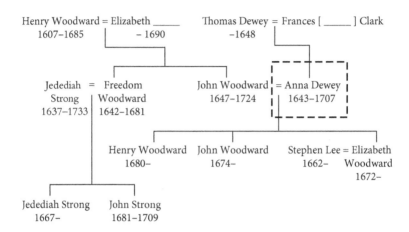

Figure 4.2.

Look next at Jedediah Strong (1637–1733). If we draw a dotted box around him, we intersect only the lines connecting him to his spouse and his children. We have yet to identify his parents. Here we have a well-defined genealogical problem. And in fact we can find a number of other genealogical problems in this chart, because every other individual is incompletely defined genealogically and thus requires further research. Thus, any partial kinship network (and that, after all, is the only type of chart we can ever draw) resembles an incomplete tapestry, with loose threads hanging out at all the edges, waiting to be woven into a larger structure.

Note further that the relationship between any two persons within the network, however complicated, whether by blood or by marriage, can be described by stringing together the appropriate selection of items from a very limited list of familial connections: parent-child, husband-wife, child-parent. Thus if we look at John Strong (1681–1709) and Henry Woodward (1680–) on the chart, we'd say they are first cousins.

Another way to state their relationship, however, is that John Strong is Henry Woodward's father's parents' son's son. Such kinship terminology is commonly used in anthropological studies, but it can help focus genealogical inquiry as well.

Any genealogical project that you can imagine may be resolved into smaller elements in the same way. If you want merely to identify a wife, or if you want to study all the agnate (male-line) descendants of a colonial immigrant, you are faced with the same problems at each step. No matter how complicated the network under study, you must be able to state reasons for saying why any person in that network is the parent, or the child, or the spouse of another. You must build up your network link by link. By remembering that you are responsible for each link, for each bond in the network, you greatly diminish your chances of going wrong.

Samuel Gay

Examine now Figure 4.3, a chart exploring the identity of the wife of Samuel Gay (1663–1753). This chart shows us that Samuel himself is completely defined genealogically. His parents and all his children are known, and we have sufficient information about his wife Abigail to include her in the chart, although her life history is not complete. If we were to demand more in calling Samuel completely defined genealogically, that is, if we were to require that the parents of Abigail be known, then we would be caught in the trap of infinite regress, for we might then

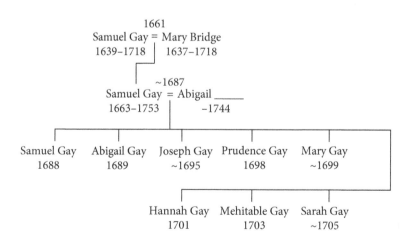

Figure 4.3.

want to be certain of the identity of Abigail's parents, and so on. Thus, each parent, spouse, and child of any person need be represented by only one independent record to make him or her an individual, who then becomes a focus for further research.

But it is Abigail, wife of Samuel, who is not genealogically defined. We know her husband and her children, but not her parents. This is one of the dangling threads on this partial kinship tapestry; this is the problem we have selected. We do have some information about Abigail. We know her age at death, so we can calculate an approximate birth year. We have extensive information about her life from 1688 until her death in 1744, but we know very little about her life before 1688, including information about her birth and her parents' identities.

This situation is one of the commonest that researchers encounter in genealogical work: we have a portion of the life history of an individual, and we are casting about for the remainder of that life—in this case, the early years of a girl named Abigail—which we can unite with the later history that we already have, to form the complete picture of a life. We possess an incomplete weaving, one of the dangling threads being Abigail, wife of Samuel Gay. We want to find another incomplete tapestry that has a dangling Abigail, and we want to find satisfactory grounds for connecting these two dangling threads, each representing a portion of the life of one individual, thus creating a larger tapestry, in which two of the dangling threads have been joined to form a complete life story, and have become part of the complete interior of the piece of art.

Our strategy will be to use the known details of the life of Abigail, wife of Samuel Gay, to identify several possible candidates for the earlier stages of this woman's life, women who might be this Abigail. We'll return to the case of Abigail Gay in Chapter Eight.[1]

Summary

Problem selection, the first step in the overall problem-solving sequence, is not a trivial matter. By drawing diagrams, and looking at each individual and each link, you are forced from the beginning to approach your genealogical work systematically and comprehensively. You accurately define the problem to be studied and the questions that are to be answered. Generally, each time you engage in genealogical work this approach to problem selection will remind you just what is meant by the solution of a genealogical problem.

Any person is **genealogically defined** if we have at least one piece of evidence that will lead to the identification of his or her parents, one piece of evidence for each spouse, and one piece of evidence for each child. Careful attention to this concept helps to further focus analytic attention on the problem at hand. Through this concept, and with the pictorial assistance of chart pedigrees, you are constantly reminded that your goal with each genealogical problem you attack is to join two partial pedigrees that were previously unconnected. The solution of any genealogical problem is in fact the solution to two reciprocal genealogical problems. This brings us to **Problem Analysis,** the second step in the problem-solving sequence and the focus of the next chapter.

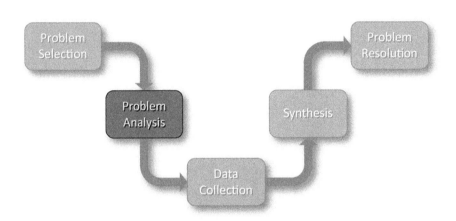

Chapter Five

Problem Analysis

Having chosen a genealogical problem to address, the next step is to analyze it to generate a plan of attack. You must at some point collect evidence that bears on the problem, but should not rush directly to that step. First, you must study the chosen problem in order to direct your search into the records in an intelligent manner. This **problem analysis** step is an important bridge between **problem selection** and **data collection**.

Three Steps of Problem Analysis

There are three parts to **problem analysis**: (1) perform a literature search; (2) analyze previous conclusions; and (3) generate a data-collection plan.

1. Perform a literature search

The first step is to seek out what pertinent work genealogical predecessors have already done. In effect, the directive is to search the literature. This may mean examining a collection of papers inherited from a relative, or perhaps a published book or article, or, in recent decades, a page on a website. Minimally, the existing literture may be nothing more than a name on a pedigree chart. This process will vary from time to time and place to place, depending on the indexes, catalogs, and other available finding aids. Much of this searching may now be done online, but on-site library research remains an essential element to this step. At the end of your literature search, you may have collected several different treatments of the family or individual of interest, frequently with discrepancies between two or more of these earlier treatments. On occasion, you will discover that all previous researchers have been in error. And in some instances you will learn that, so far as the public record is concerned, no one has done previous work on this problem.

2. Analyze previous conclusions

Once you have this material in hand, you can dissect it to determine what evidence has already been collected, and attempt to understand earlier researchers' thought processes. In other words, you perform a reverse version of linkage analysis, beginning with the conclusions, and attempting to untangle and delineate the linkage decisions that were made to arrive at these conclusions. And you may have to regress even further and assess the record analysis and source analysis steps taken by earlier researchers.

3. Generate a data collection plan

Once you have performed the **reverse linkage analysis,** you will be in a position to construct a plan for gathering the evidence you will need for synthesis and resolution, the final two stages of the problem-solving sequence. First, you may discover that you need to reexamine the evidence already considered by previous researchers. Perhaps you suspect that earlier researchers inaccurately reported this evidence, or that they failed to seek out a more reliable version of that same evidence. Second, you may believe that there are sources never examined by earlier researchers that may hold useful records of importance to the problem in front of you. The last stage in problem analysis is the construction of a list of sources to be examined (or reexamined). The actual research based on that list will be the subject of the next chapter, on data collection.

Sample Problem Analyses

The three new examples in this chapter explore the process of problem analysis. In each case, we will carry through the remainder of the steps of the problem-solving sequence and complete our work on these problems in this chapter, thus getting a preview of the material in the remaining three chapters.

Jose Glover

Let's begin with a relatively simple example of revisiting the research of an earlier scholar. Writing in 1869, in an attempt to establish the correct form of the given name of an early New England settler, John W. Dean observed the following in an article in *The New England Historical and Genealogical Register,* "Rev. Joseph or Josse Glover":

> The Christian name of Rev. Mr. Glover . . . is variously given, by different writers, viz., *Joseph, Josse* and *Jesse.* The latter is evidently an error arising from mistaking an *o* for a round *e.* Mr. Savage decides in favor of the singular if not unique name of Josse; but Miss Anna Glover, in her *Glover Memorials and Genealogies,* produces very strong evidence in favor of Joseph. The name is Joseph on a monument erected, in 1629, by Mr. Glover himself, to the memory of his first wife, who died July 10, 1628; it is so on the register of Sutton in Surrey, England, of which parish he was the rector from 1628 to 1636; and it is so also in Winthrop's journal. On the other hand, it is written Josse in several instances on the Suffolk Registry of Deeds, as well as in the will printed below. This may be intended for an abbreviation of Joseph, though it would be an unusual one.[1]

In this brief passage, Dean is engaged in problem analysis. He has sought out two earlier discussions of the problem of the given name of Rev. Glover, one prepared by James Savage and the other by Anna Glover. Dean then analyzes a handful of records bearing on the problem, including a monumental inscription, a parish register, and Winthrop's journal. We cannot tell for all of these whether Dean is simply commenting on the records as presented by Savage and Glover, or whether he has sought out these pieces of evidence on his own.

Seven years later, in 1876, J. Hammond Trumbull addressed this same problem, listing a number of authors who had settled variously on Joseph, Jesse, or Josse for Rev. Glover's given name. Whereas most of his predecessors had relied on published sources for their conclusions, Trumbull systematically sought out the original of each record.

> The strongest evidence I have found for *Jesse* is in the printed Calendar of British State Papers (Dom. Series, 1634–35), in the abstracts of a petition addressed to Archbishop Laud by Edward Darcey, patron of the living of Sutton, for appointment of a successor to "Jesse Glover, clerk," and of Laud's answer to this petition, in which this name is repeated (p. 355, doc. 45). . . . For *Joseph*, the authorities are the printed extracts from the College Records, and the Sutton inscription printed by Manning and Bray. Mr. Sibley, having at my request examined the MS. Record of Donations quoted by Peirce and Quincy, gives me the extract *literatim*:
>
> > "Mr. *Joss:* Glover gave to the College a font of printing letters."
>
> Suspecting that Manning and Bray had taken the same liberty in copying the inscription on the monument erected by Mr. Glover to his first wife, as had been taken in printing extracts from the college records, I applied to the present rector of Sutton, a well known scholar and antiquary, the Rev. John A. Gilles, D.D. He very obligingly complied with my request, by informing me that the name on the monument is "Jos. Glover" — not "Joseph," and that the entry in the register, of which he sends me a certified copy, is *Jose*.
>
> This disposes of all the authority for "Joseph."
>
> For the correction of "Jesse," in the printed Calendar of State Papers, I addressed an inquiry to William Douglas Hamilton, Esq., F.S.A., who succeeds the late Mr. Bruce as editor of this series of the Calendars. He favors me with the following reply:
>
> > In reply to your note of the 18th ult., I can only say that I have looked carefully at the documents you mentioned, and find that the name is clearly written as you suggested, *Josse Glover*, both in the body of the petition and in Archbishop Laud's reference at the bottom of the petition.
>
> There is then, so far as appears, no contemporary authority for either *Joseph* or *Jesse*. All the record evidence favors *Josse* or *Jose*.[2]

Trumbull relieved Dean's confusion over Rev. Glover's given name by taking his research one step further, arranging for the examination of the original of each of the documents in question. In other words, as part of his problem analysis, Trumbull decided that reliance on the evidence as already collected and published was not sufficient. Having gathered the evidence according to his data collection plan, he demonstrated—as shown in the lengthy passage quoted above—that each of the records that purported to give the name as Jesse or Joseph actually had Josse or some close variant thereof.

Authors prior to Trumbull had linked a number of records that they thought belonged to one man, Rev. Glover. Because of the uncertainty attached to the given name of this minister, however, the possibility remained open that one or more of these records might pertain to a different individual; that is, that one or more of the linkage decisions made by earlier authors was incorrect. By resolving the discrepancies surrounding the name Jose, Trumbull validated and strengthened these earlier linkage decisions, demonstrating that all these records pertained to the same man.

Both Dean and Trumbull engaged in problem analysis. Their work confirmed the original conclusion, made by Anna Glover, that all the records under consideration belonged to the same individual. They demonstrated, however, that she had come to an incorrect conclusion as to that person's given name. Trumbull probed deeper than did Dean, and—a better problem analyst than Dean—he was thereby able to reach a more certain conclusion.

Abigail Powell

Another good example arises from the study of the family of Michael Powell of Dedham and Boston, Massachusetts. Michael and Abigail (Bedle) Powell had seven known children, of whom the youngest was Abigail, probably born about 1651. By directly studying the Powell family, we learn relatively little of Abigail's fate. Her father died intestate, and nothing is said about any of his children in the few papers in his probate file. Her mother did leave a will, dated 14 March 1676/7, in which she made many bequests, including one to "my four daughters," one of whom is listed as Abigail Howlett, and another bequest to Samuel Howlett, with no relationship stated.[3] We are looking, then, for a Howlett male who had a wife Abigail by 1676, probably but not necessarily living in the Boston area; this man's name may be Samuel, or else he and Abigail may have had a son Samuel.

The first step is to perform a literature search. By using the bibliographic aids available to us, in this case Clarence Almon Torrey's *New England Marriages Prior to 1700*, one of the items we discover is *The Ancestry of Dudley Wildes*, published in 1959, one of the last of the series of sixteen "great-great-grandparent" volumes researched and compiled by Walter Goodwin Davis. This volume contains a section on a John Howlett of Boston. The list of children for that man includes a Samuel born in Boston on 6 February 1672/3. The place and the date fit the description of the person we are looking for. Has Davis already done our work for us?

We proceed to the second step, reverse linkage analysis. The first clue that something does not fit is that Davis states that the wife of this John Howlett was Susanna Hudson, daughter of Francis Hudson of Boston, whereas we are looking for a Howlett who married a daughter of Michael Powell. The John Howlett treated by Davis died by 1675, and his wife remarried twice and survived into the eighteenth century. The sketch created by Davis gives this couple two children in addition to Samuel, a daughter Mary born in 1670, and a daughter Sarah born in 1674. If Susanna Hudson was the mother of all three of these children, then this John Howlett cannot be the man who married Abigail Powell.

Having reached this conclusion, we proceed to building a data collection plan. This consists simply of going back to the Boston vital records, to confirm the details of the births of the three children Davis assigned to this couple. The three birth records, as published, are the following:

> Mary of John & Susanna Howlet born Jan. 22 [1670][4]
> Samuel of John & Abigail Howlet born Feb. 6 [1672][5]
> Sarah of John & Susanna Howlet born May 22 [1674][6]

Now we can return to the second step in problem analysis, the reverse linkage analysis, in an attempt to recreate Davis's reasoning. In his treatment of the Howlett family, Davis did not provide his rationale for linking each of these births to the same set of parents, John and Susanna (Hudson) Howland. He simply listed the three births, without noting the discrepancy in the name of the mother given for the second child. Davis was too careful a researcher to have missed this detail. A likely explanation is that he assumed a simple clerical error. After all, the three dates fall in a typical sequence, with approximately two-year intervals between births, and with no other records for children born to a John Howlett found in Boston, or anywhere else in New England, in the 1660s, 1670s, and 1680s.

Clearly, Davis was not aware of the evidence from the will of Michael Powell's widow, or he would not have made the linkage decisions he did. Based on what we know now, though, we must question this set of linkage decisions. The outcome of problem analysis in this case is that we need to collect more information on the name John Howlett in hopes of resolving this discrepancy.

Returning to the literature search step, we find that in 1913 John William Linzee collected and abstracted many records for John Howlett in *The History of Peter Parker and Sarah Ruggles of Roxbury, Mass., and Their Ancestors and Descendants.*[7] Linzee agreed with Davis that John Howlett, son of Thomas, married Susanna Hudson. Because this John Howlett and his wife were not in the main line of descent Linzee was following, he did not attempt to identify all the children of this couple. Linzee did produce documents that show that this John Howlett had died by 26 January 1675/6, when his probate inventory was produced at court.[8]

Also, on 15 June 1676, "Susanna Howlet relict widow of John Howlet late of Boston in New England mariner deceased" sold land in Boston.[9] On 31 July 1677, the remaining estate of "John Howlett mariner late of Boston deceased" was "equally divided between Susanna his relict & Mary his only child."[10] Soon after the division of the estate, the widow Susanna remarried to Edmund Perkins, for on 8 May 1678 Edmund Perkins, son of Edmund and Susanna Perkins, was born at Boston.[11]

Linzee was in agreement with Walter Goodwin Davis that a John Howlett married Susanna Hudson, daughter of Francis Hudson, and died in late 1675 or early 1676. No fault is found with the linkage decisions made by Linzee in connecting the deeds and probate records for John and Susanna (Hudson) Howlett.

We are still left, however, with the discrepancy of the 1672 birth record for a Samuel Howlett, son of John and Abigail, and the fact that this is the only Samuel Howlett who might match up with the Samuel named in the will of Abigail (Bedle) Powell.

So, despite both Davis's and Linzee's acknowledged thoroughness, we return to the third step of problem analysis, expanding our data collection plan to encompass a search of all Massachusetts Bay records for the latter part of the seventeenth century for any appearance of the name John Howlett. Further exploration of Suffolk County deeds shows that Linzee did not publish all records for the name John Howlett in Boston for this time period. On 18 August 1679, "John Howlet of Boston in the Colony of Massachusets in New England mariner & Abigail his wife" sold land in Boston near the North Battery.[12]

The John Howlett who had married Susanna Hudson had already been dead for more than three years, and his widow had been remarried for nearly two, by the date of this 1679 deed. Clearly there were two John Howletts in Boston in the 1670s, both of whom were mariners (thus adding to the confusion). Knowing this, we complete the problem analysis phase of our work on this problem, and we proceed to synthesis and resolution.

We may now state that Walter Goodwin Davis was in error in linking the 6 February 1672 birth of a Samuel Howlett in Boston to the family of John and Susanna (Hudson) Howlett. This newly freed record may now be linked to the 1679 deed for John Howlett and wife Abigail given just above, thus creating a small linkage bundle (Figure 5.1). It forms the beginning of a dossier for a second John Howlett family.

Finally, we have now come full circle, having demonstrated that there was a male Howlett in Boston who meets the criteria for being the husband of Abigail Powell, daughter of Michael Powell. John and Abigail (Powell) Howlett had

Samuel, son of John and Abigail Howlett, was born at Boston on 6 February 1672[/3].

On 18 August 1679, "John Howlet of Boston . . . , mariner, & Abigail his wife" sold to Richard Shute of Boston a parcel of land "in Boston aforesaid near unto the North Battery."

Conclusion: A John Howlett with wife Abigail resided in Boston from at least 1672 to 1679. In 1672 this couple had a son Samuel. This John Howlett was distinct from another John Howlett with wife Susanna who also resided at Boston during some of this same period.

Rationale: A previous researcher had linked the birth record for Samuel to the family of the John Howlett with wife Susanna, apparently believing that there was only one John Howlett in Boston at the time. Closer examination of the birth record for Samuel showed that his mother's name was Abigail, not Susanna. This might have been written off as a clerical error, were it not for the fact that the John Howlett with wife Susanna had died by 1676, whereas the 1679 deed shows that a John Howlett with wife Abigail was alive after that date. Thus, there must have been at least two adult John Howletts in Boston in the 1670s. Finally, for the two records presented above not to pertain to the same John Howlett, we would have to postulate a third John Howlett, for which there is no evidence.

Confidence: Highly probable.

Figure 5.1.

son Samuel born in Boston in 1672, and this son would have been the Samuel Howlett named in the will of Michael Powell's widow.[13]

This case required us to loop back through the steps of the problem analysis procedure twice, performing all three steps a second time before being ready to proceed to a full solution of the problem.

Stephen Farr

On occasion the examination of the work of earlier researchers will reveal a genealogical phantom: a person who never actually existed. This may occur when a genealogist has linked a number of records to create an individual, but closer examination reveals that each of these records has been misinterpreted in some way, or the records may themselves be simply defective in some manner, or the records may pertain to some other individual who actually did exist.

In 1996 the Winslow Farr Sr. Family Organization wanted to trace the ancestry of Stephen Farr, who appeared at Concord, Massachusetts, in 1674, when he married Mary Taylor. According to the genealogical literature, Stephen Farr was son of Thomas Farr, who was recorded in Massachusetts as early as 1645. The entire career of this alleged Thomas Farr comprised three scattered records.

1. Earlier researchers stated that a record of Thomas Farr had been found in Boston in 1645, but they did not identify this record. The only record so far discovered that might match this claim is a power of attorney, dated 2 January 1644/5, from "Tho[mas] Farrar of Boston husbandman (son of Thomas Farrar of or near Burnley in Lanc[ashir]e husbandman) unto Henry Farrar his brother mariner."[14] Assuming that this is the record previous researchers intended, it provides no evidence for the existence of a Thomas Farr, but of a Thomas Farrar, a distinct surname.

2. On 6 November 1654, "Mr. Dan[ie]ll King in New-england & County of Essex" sold to "Tho[mas] Farr of the same place" several parcels of land in the town of Lynn, nearly 100 acres in all.[15] Daniel King was a well-documented resident of Lynn from about 1640 until his death there in 1672. No other record has been found for a Thomas Farr in Lynn, which would be surprising for someone who had acquired that much land. There was, however, a Thomas Farrar who lived in Lynn from about 1640 until 1694, and this man is almost certainly the grantee in the deed from Daniel King.

3. "Thomas Farr" is named in an undated deposition from Suffolk County, Massachusetts, court files.[16] Other persons named in the same deposition were Ebenezer Parkhurst and his wife Mary, and Thomas Powers. Ebenezer Parkhurst lived at Chelmsford, Massachusetts, and married Mary about 1695. Thomas Powers resided at nearby Concord and married sometime in the early 1690s. Stephen Farr was also an inhabitant of Concord, and he had a son Thomas born about 1688. The likely resolution then, is that this deposition was made in the early 1700s, and the Thomas Farr named therein was the son of Stephen, and not the putative father.

The earlier researchers had taken these three records and linked them to form one man, whom they then identified as the father of Stephen Farr. This linkage was apparently made solely because (the researchers thought) the name Thomas Farr appeared in all three, and all three, scattered as they were, placed this man in eastern Massachusetts.

Through our record-by-record analysis above, however, we see that two of the records were very probably for a Thomas Farrar, rather than Farr, and the third was for a son of Stephen Farr, not the father. There are, in fact, no records for a Thomas Farr in New England in the generation prior to Stephen Farr. We have performed the ultimate act of reverse linkage analysis, peeling away all the records thought to pertain to a Thomas Farr and demonstrating that there was no such person.

This name now becomes an empty husk, a genealogical phantom, and should be removed from the Farr pedigree. As mentioned in the preceding chapter, *for a name to appear on a genealogical chart, at least one verified, reliable, contemporary record for that name must exist.* In the case of Stephen Farr, no such record has been found that might pertain to his father, whatever the name of his father might have been. On a pedigree chart for Stephen Farr, the slot for his father's name should be blank.[17]

Genealogical phantoms make frequent appearances, and on occasion entire books have been written about the descendants of such non-entities. In 1895, Francis Constantine Hill compiled and published *Biographical Sketch and Genealogical Record of the Descendants of Melanchthon Hill, of Connecticut, 1610 to 1895.* The author had found a 1642 birth record at Hartford, Connecticut, for a son of a man named Lank Hill. Unable to believe that Lank could be an acceptable given name at that time and place, the author concluded that it must be an abbreviated form for Melanchthon, in honor of the sixteenth-century Reformation minister Philip Melanchthon. Proceeding on that basis, he then traced the descendants of the son born in 1642. What the author failed to notice was that there were many other records in early Hartford for a man named Luke Hill, and the 1642 birth record had been misread by someone, "Luke" being misinterpreted as "Lank." Lank, or Melanchthon, Hill never existed.

Summary

The **problem analysis** stage in the problem-solving sequence consists of three steps:

1. Perform a literature search.
2. Analyze previous conclusions (undertake **reverse linkage analysis**).
3. Generate a **data collection** plan.

By carrying out this three-step program, you may be certain that you fully understand the status of the problem you are analyzing, the work that has been done by previous genealogists. This allows you to move along to a careful and complete plan for collecting any additional information you may need to proceed to generate your own genealogical conclusions, a process that we will address in the next two chapters.

During this stage you are, in a sense, moving backward. You are stepping down from a level of conclusions made by earlier researchers, from the proofs of genealogical conclusions they made, and returning briefly to the lower stratum of raw evidence. You may find that your predecessors inaccurately presented or incorrectly interpreted some of the evidence, or you may come across new evidence they did not see. Take this journey back from proof to evidence with a view either to confirm the work of others or to improve on their work and come to broader and sounder conclusions.

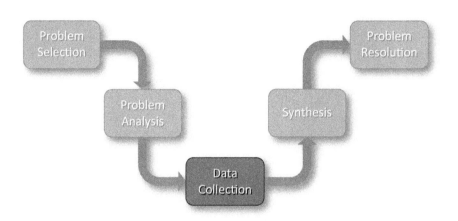

Chapter Six

Data Collection

As part of the problem analysis step, we identified a number of **data collection** goals. Now it's time to put your research plan into action, either by revisiting records already examined by others, or by collecting records from sources not previously exploited.

First, you may find that a number of the records cited by previous researchers require reexamination. This may be because you have some doubts about the accuracy of the record as presented by the previous researcher, or because you have only an extract or abstract available for analysis, and would like the whole record. Beyond this, you may wish to look at the source from which the record is drawn because you believe that it contains additional relevant records.

Second, you may feel that you need to explore sources that the previous researchers did not consider. Such sources may have been unknown to the previous researcher, or may have been discovered or made more readily available since the time of the earlier work.

Data Collection Toolkit

For the data collection step in the problem-solving sequence, you need four assorted tools:

You will need the appropriate finding-aids for locating sources.

You will need to seek out the **specific external knowledge** pertinent to your problem.

You will need to determine the **record density** for the time and place you are researching.

You will need to take care that the records you collect are **accurately reported** and **carefully documented.**

Locating Sources

First, you need to know where to find the sources. Different times and places create different ranges of source material, with the result that you need specialized local knowledge in this step. Dozens if not hundreds of publications might assist you in this task. Here is a small sample:

- For many years the best guide to the locations of records of genealogical value was a two-volume set first published by the American Society of Genealogists in 1960 (with an updated edition issued in 1980) and edited by Milton Rubincam and Jean Stephenson: *Genealogical Research: Methods and Sources* (known to many affectionately, if irreverently, as GeRMS). The volumes begin with a few general chapters on genealogical research methodology, followed by several chapters organized by record type, then several more arranged by state or region of the United States. Finally, there are a few chapters on records in Europe and Canada.

- The next important volume in this mode to appear was Val D. Greenwood's *The Researcher's Guide to American Genealogy* [Baltimore; Genealogical Publishing Co., 1974]. This guide opens with seven chapters on "Background to Research," mostly about the mechanics of the research process. The remainder of the book comprises seventeen chapters under the heading "Records and Their Use," covering vital records, censuses, probate records, land records, and the like. The first edition of Greenwood's work was published just before the explosion of interest in genealogy pursuant to the U.S. Bicentennial and the publication of, and later broadcast of the miniseries of, Alex Haley's *Roots*. Accordingly, it has been widely used and is still valuable.

- A decade later Ancestry Publishing Company (now Ancestry.com) published *The Source: A Guidebook of American Genealogy*, edited by Arlene Eakle and Johni Cerny [Salt Lake City: Ancestry Publishing Co., 1984]. After an introductory chapter on "Genealogical Records and Techniques," the bulk of this book consists of chapters on "Major Record Sources" and "Published Genealogical Sources," covering all the usual categories. The volume concludes with half a dozen chapters on research in various ethnic groups. This publication to some extent supplanted Greenwood, and has run through three print editions. In 1997 and 2006 Loretto Dennis Szucs and Sandra Hargreaves Luebking prepared second and third editions of this volume, with much new material.

Specific External Knowledge

Having located the sources of interest, we then need to know how to interpret them. All sources and records we encounter, from whatever jurisdiction, will be susceptible to the analytic tools described above in Chapters One through Three, supplemented by generic external knowledge. In addition, however, we must have the specialized local knowledge referred to above.

Specific external knowledge, mentioned earlier, and particularly in Chapter Three, covers material that varies from place to place and time to time. Such knowledge may concern such matters as the laws and customs of marriage, or the procedures by which various government bodies distribute land to individuals. A vast literature is necessary to cover this part of genealogical research; unfortunately, not all of that literature has yet been created.

For example, it would be helpful to have, for each state and colony, a volume discussing in detail the laws and customs of that jurisdiction as they apply to genealogical research. One such volume, specifically for the state of North Carolina, should be a model for all others in this genre: Helen F. M. Leary and Maurice R. Stirewalt, eds., *North Carolina Research: Genealogy and Local History,* 2nd ed. (Raleigh: North Carolina Genealogical Society, 1996). The editors present their material in forty-five chapters, organized in six groups: Research Techniques, County Records, State Records, Federal Records, Private Records, and Nonwritten Records.

The value of Leary and Stirewalt's approach is evident in the first three chapters in the County Records section: Marriage, Divorce, and Vital Statistics; Wills; and Estates Records. Each of these chapters describes the different types of records that may be found in each of these categories, such as marriage bonds, licenses, and registers; the three types of wills; and estate documents such as inventories, accounts, and settlements. Moreover, each of these three chapters begins with a section explaining how these records are created: "Laws and Customs Affecting Marriage"; "The Nature of Wills"; and "Settling Estates." By setting forth the details peculiar to North Carolina in the creation of each of these record types, Leary and Stirewalt not only direct us to the locations of these sources, but also prepare us for the source analysis and record analysis steps once we have gathered our data.

In your own research you will need to acquire the specific external knowledge pertinent to your problem, time frame, and geographic area.

Record Density

A guiding principle in both the collection and the analysis of data is the concept of **record density**. This term refers to the variability in the density of sources and records available to you from time to time and place to place. Record density is determined by three variables:

1. The variety of types of sources created
2. The number of those sources that have survived
3. The completeness of coverage of each of those sources

Record density may vary widely from place to place at all jurisdictional levels—whether town, county, colony, state, or country—and within each jurisdiction from one time period to another. It will determine not only the sources available to you but the choices you will make during data collection. For a time and place with high record density, you may begin your research by examining only a few source types known to be of high genealogical value. For a time and place with low record density, you may need to search every available source.

In early New England, for example, with its emphasis on the town, the common practice was for the town to maintain records of town meetings, grants of land, and vital events; for the church to keep registers of baptisms, burials, admissions, and dismissions; and for the county to record deeds and probate records. Not all of these records were consistently kept, however, and those that were may not have survived. (The Puritan immigrants to New England allowed marriage as a civil ceremony only, so church records do not include marriages until late in the seventeenth century. In all the New England colonies, the earliest deeds were recorded at the town level; this arrangement was retained in Connecticut, Rhode Island, and [later] in Vermont, whereas counties were soon established in Massachusetts Bay and the recording of deeds slowly transferred to that jurisdictional level.)

At Dedham, Massachusetts, in its early decades, for example, the town, church, and vital records were maintained and have survived. By contrast, the town of Lynn, Massachusetts, founded just a few years before Dedham, presumably created a similar set of records for the early decades, but none have survived. County records of deeds and probates survive for both towns. As a result, research on Dedham families is simpler and more rewarding than Lynn research. For Lynn families, the researcher has to lean more heavily on the county and colony records. (*Note:* A smattering of entries from the Lynn town records survive in the form of extracts made for court proceedings. They can be found in the loose papers of the Essex County courts.)

Even when a given category of records was maintained for a given jurisdiction and has survived, the coverage of that source was not always complete. In Boston, Massachusetts, for instance, the completeness of the recording of births, marriages, and deaths varies widely throughout the colonial period. William Aspinwall was Boston town clerk from 1643 until his departure for England in 1652. For a few years he performed his duties well, compiling the Boston Book of Possessions and recording the vital records. He began to neglect his work in 1647, however, and by 1651 he was gathering records for only a small fraction of the vital events occurring in Boston.[1]

Turning to another time and place, efforts to uncover the English origins of seventeenth-century immigrants to North America rely heavily on the parish registers and probate records of England in the early years of that century and the later years of the sixteenth century. These two categories of records have survived well for many parts of England. In the East Anglian counties of Essex, Suffolk, and Norfolk, the source for many of the earliest settlers of New England, probate records are nearly complete and relatively few parish registers have been lost. In the West Country, however, another important source region for migration to the New World, the surviving resources are not as complete. At the onset of World War II, British authorities moved much archival material to locations that were supposedly more secure than their natural homes. Unfortunately, the probate records of the diocese of Exeter, covering Cornwall and Devonshire, were destroyed by German bombing in 1942. (Prior to 1838, probate was handled by the church courts.) This gap in the sources may be partially filled by seeking out copies of probate documents made by researchers prior to 1942. Many wills from the diocese of Exeter were abstracted and published by Henry F. Waters in *Genealogical Gleanings in England* (2 volumes; Boston, 1901). In addition, Olive M. Moger abstracted thousands of wills from the same source, now preserved in forty-four typescript volumes, available at the Family History Library in Salt Lake City. These collections of abstracts do not completely fill the gap left by the destruction of 1942, but they are far better than nothing.

The concept of **record density** helps the researcher not only during the data collection process but also in later stages of the problem-solving sequence. When attempting to determine the identity of a wife when you have a given name and an approximate age, it can be helpful to search the records of the known residence of the family at about the time of the marriage, collecting all birth and baptismal records for women of that given name within a stated range of years. (See the case study of the search for the wife of Samuel Gay as presented in Chapters Four and Eight.) Your confidence in reaching a satisfactory conclusion in such cases increases proportionally with the increasing record density for that time and place, as there is less chance of missing a potential candidate spouse.

Accurately Reported and Carefully Documented

The Overview set forth two compact rules for doing genealogical research. The first two parts of the First Fundamental Rule speak directly to the data collection process:

> All statements must be based only on *accurately reported, carefully documented,* and exhaustively analyzed records.

Accurately Reported

Whether you choose to present the record as a transcript, extract, or abstract, you must do so with the greatest accuracy possible. An error at this earliest stage in the process will reverberate throughout your later work, and every effort you make now to minimize errors will pay dividends as the problem-solving sequence proceeds. (Note the relevance here of the second question posed in the chapter on source analysis: *Is it the original or a copy?* In the present context, however, you are concerned with preparation for the form in which you will present your conclusions to future researchers. Your goal is to present the material in such a way that it will stand up to future practitioners of source analysis who are using your work.)

Furthermore, as noted above, one of the results of your problem analysis may be that you question a record as presented in earlier work. One of the goals in your own work should be to give those who follow you as little reason as possible to reexamine the records you present. A good checklist of the steps to be taken in making an accurate record of your gathered data has been presented in the section "Data-Collection Standards" in *The BCG Genealogical Standards Manual*.[2]

Carefully Documented

Because there will be occasions when future researchers want to check your work (just as you did in the problem analysis stage), you must be certain that your research is "carefully documented." A number of systems of documentation or source citation have been published. We commend two very simple principles for documentation:

- Documentation should be clear.
- Documentation should be consistent.

Clear means (1) that any titles, repositories, abbreviations, or other elements of the citation be understandable by other researchers (whether directly or through a key), and (2) that the citation will allow other researchers to find the source, and the record in the source, with minimum effort.

Consistent means (1) that multiple citations to the same source use the same form, and (2) that citations to similar sources be of similar form. This will obviously aid in helping other researchers to follow the work you have done. (Of course, the first occurrence of a given source may be presented in full and subsequent references to that same source may be abbreviated, but that abbreviated form should still be consistent.)

Two of the greatest genealogists of recent decades have published three important volumes on the procedures for citation of sources:

- In 1980 Richard S. Lackey, FASG, published *Cite Your Sources: A Manual for Documenting Family Histories and Genealogical Records* [New Orleans 1980]. Lackey provides sound guidance for the task of creating citations, and follows up his guiding principles with many illustrative examples.

- In 1997 Elizabeth Shown Mills, FASG, published *Evidence! Citation & Analysis for the Family Historian* [Baltimore 1997]. Mills covers similar ground as Lackey, but she adds a chapter on analysis of the data, in addition to citation of sources. Moreover, she tackles the problem of citing online and other electronic sources.

- Just ten years later, in 2007, Mills expanded her work extensively, to more than eight hundred pages, with the new title *Evidence Explained: Citing History Sources from Artifacts to Cyberspace* [Baltimore 2007]. This expanded version of Mills's work adds twelve pages to the chapter on data analysis and elaborates at great length on the forms of citation, providing hundreds of detailed examples of both print and electronic source citations.

Summary

Unlike the other steps in the problem-solving sequence, **data collection** is driven by the variability of source creation across time and place, and so is not susceptible to a single procedure. It has been treated best and most extensively in the existing literature.

As part of the data collection process, we discussed four tools that are needed for this step. First, you must know how to locate the sources of interest to you. Second, you must be able to locate the **specific external knowledge** relevant to the problem under consideration. Third, you must be attentive to the **record density** for the time and place being researched. Fourth, you must ensure that the records you are collecting are **accurately reported** and **carefully documented.**

Having completed data collection, it is time for the fourth step in the problem-solving sequence, **synthesis**, in which you begin the process of linking up your bits of evidence, on the way to your goal of arriving at a new genealogical conclusion.

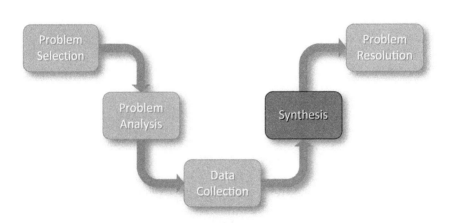

Chapter Seven

Synthesis

Chapter Three, **Linkage Analysis,** described the process of determining whether two or more records pertain to the same individual. In that discussion we looked at examples in which two or more records were examined and then linked, with greater or lesser confidence in the conclusions in each case. Those examples were dealing with one locality and a limited time frame, generally comprising only a small portion of the full biography of the person of interest. In that first level of **linkage analysis** we created **linkage bundles**.

Now, in the **synthesis** step of the problem-solving sequence, we take linkage analysis to the next level by examining two or more of these linkage bundles, which we suspect pertain to the same person. The goal is to provide a **rationale** for linking two or more linkage bundles into the broader construct of a **dossier,** thus creating a fuller description of an individual's life.

We present here four examples of connecting two or more **linkage bundles** into a **dossier**. The first two examples are new examples, in which we will trace all steps of the problem-solving sequence, but with emphasis on the Synthesis stage. The first example is one in which we are unable to reach a firm conclusion, while the second example is selected especially to illustrate the Synthesis step. Following these two examples, we return to two of our ongoing case studies and bring them both to a conclusion.

> ### Example One: Hannah Farnham, insufficient evidence

Let's examine the marriage at Haverhill, Massachusetts, on 26 December 1650 of Abraham Tyler and Hannah Farnham, focusing on Hannah and the completion of her genealogical definition. The marriage record identifies her spouse as of 1650. Who were her parents? What children did she have with Abraham Tyler? Did she have any other husbands? Although we will provide partial answers to all these questions, the problem we have selected to solve is the identity of her parents.

Problem analysis is minimal in this instance, as nothing of substance has been published about Abraham Tyler. Our data collection plan involves nothing more complicated than scouring the records of Essex County, Massachusetts, for appearances of Abraham and Hannah Tyler.

We begin by creating a linkage bundle for Hannah Farnham as wife and later widow of Abraham Tyler. Abraham Tyler died at Haverhill on 6 May 1673. In his will of 5 May 1673, Abraham Tyler bequeathed 20 acres of land to "Robert Clement the son of Robert Clements" and the rest of his estate to "my loving wife." "Hannah Tiler, widow of Abraham," presented the will at court on 14 October 1673.[1] Records for Abraham Tyler are quite sparse, and nothing in the few surviving records indicates that there was more than one man of the name in New England in the latter half of the seventeenth century. Thus, the Hannah Tyler of 1673, widow of Abraham, is almost certainly the same woman as the Hannah Farnham who married Abraham Tyler in 1650. Our linkage bundle consists of the 1650 marriage record for Hannah Farnham and Abraham Tyler and the 1673 probate record naming "Hannah Tiler, widow of Abraham." With only two records we have encompassed twenty-three years in the life of this woman, and identified a spouse. (See Figure 7.1.)

What became of Hannah, widow of Abraham Tyler? No marriage or death record for her has been found. A search of various Essex County,

---

Linkage Bundle: Hannah Farnham no. 1

On 26 December 1650, Abraham Tyler and Hannah Farnham were married at Haverhill, Massachusetts

On 14 October 1673, "Hannah Tiler, widow of Abraham," presented the will of "Abraham Tyler of Haverhill" for probate

Conclusion: Hannah Farnham who married Abraham Tyler in 1650 is identical with "Hannah Tiler, widow of Abraham," in 1673.

Rationale: The names Abraham and Hannah provide the principal points of comparison. Records for Abraham Tyler are quite sparse, and nothing in the few surviving records indicates that there was more than one man of the name in New England in the latter half of the seventeenth century. We employ here the concept of Record Density. The deed and probate records for Essex County survive for this period, and the vital records for Haverhill are reasonably complete. Had there been more than two men by the name of Abraham Tyler in Haverhill, or indeed in Essex County, in the third quarter of the seventeenth century, the surviving records should have provided some hint that there was a second Abraham.

Confidence: Almost certain.

Figure 7.1.

Massachusetts, sources turns up one record that apparently pertains to her: a deed indicating that on 28 September 1695, "Hannah Brumidge of Haverhill . . . formerly the wife of Abraham Tiler being his relict widow," in return for maintenance for the remainder of her life, conveyed to John White "the homestead formerly Abraham Tyler's abovesaid." The deed was signed by Edward Brumidge and Hannah Brumidge, and acknowledged on 13 January 1700/1 by "widow Hannah Brumidge."[2]

For the moment, let's examine this record in isolation. We have a woman named Hannah, claiming in 1695 that she was now wife of Edward Brumidge but had formerly been wife of Abraham Tyler. Six years later, she acknowledges her 1695 act, now describing herself as "widow Hannah Brumidge." Although the 28 September 1695 and 13 January 1700/1 events occur adjacent to one another, in the same document, we may consider them as two records, separated as the two events are by six years. Trivial as it may seem, we have here another linkage bundle, the two records being the deed itself and the acknowledgement six years later. This little linkage bundle (Figure 7.2) encompasses the life of a woman named Hannah who in 1695 was married to Edward Brumidge, her second husband, but who by 1701 was a widow.

To this point we have deliberately ignored the part of the 1695 deed in which Hannah Brumidge, wife of Edward, explicitly stated that she had earlier been

---

Linkage Bundle: Hannah Farnham no. 2

On 28 September 1695, "Hannah Brumidge of Haverhill … formerly the wife of Abraham Tiler being his relict widow" arranged with John White for her maintenance for life; the deed was signed by Edward Brumidge and Hannah Brumidge

On 13 January 1700/1, this deed was acknowledged by "widow Hannah Brumidge"

Conclusion: By 28 September 1695, Edward Brumidge had married a woman named Hannah. By 13 January 1700/1, this same Hannah was now a widow.

Rationale: The reasoning behind the joining of these two records is quite simple. The acknowledgement of 13 January 1700/1 is appended directly to the deed of 28 September 1695. Barring an extraordinary clerical blunder, the person making the acknowledgement must be the same as the grantor of the deed. (This argument has much the same logic as the phenomenon of internal back-references as seen in the Winthrop Medical Journal.)

Confidence: Almost certain.

Figure 7.2.

married to Abraham Tyler. Again, as trivial as it may seem, we must consciously and deliberately place the two linkage bundles next to one another, to see if they may be combined into a more complex, higher-level structure, a **dossier**. The point of comparison, the common thread, is the name Abraham Tyler. If we had evidence of more than one man of this name in New England in the latter half of the seventeenth century, the task could become very difficult. However, examination of a wide range of New England records does not uncover anyone else named Abraham Tyler. More specifically, the first linkage bundle tells us that Abraham Tyler married Hannah Farnham at Haverhill and died there more than twenty years later, while the second linkage bundle tells us that the Hannah who in 1695 was married to Edward Brumidge, but had earlier been married to an Abraham Tyler, was residing in Haverhill. The Abraham Tyler of the first linkage bundle was dead by the time of the second linkage bundle. There are, then, no impediments to concluding that the Hannah of the first linkage bundle is the same person as the Hannah of the second linkage bundle. This may seem an excess of effort to reach what seems to be an obvious result. And in many instances you will make such connections without pausing for much reflection. But the failure to make this analytic effort all too often leads to incorrect linkages, and may remain buried and unexamined at the base of research for many years. By paying attention to such simple linkages at every step in your research, you will build a stronger foundation for a pedigree.

With just three records (a marriage record, a probate case, and a deed—which is actually two records, as we have seen above), we have created a small but reasonably solid dossier for Hannah (Farnham) (Tyler) Brumidge, tracing her from her marriage in 1650 to her second widowhood in 1701. Figure 7.3 diagrams the formation of this dossier.

The typical dossier diagram resembles linkage bundle diagrams, but with an extra layer of encapsulation. As with linkage bundle diagrams, the innermost elements consist of the pieces of evidence, again in unshaded rectangular boxes. This evidence is contained within the linkage bundle, which provides the conclusions, the rationale for those conclusions and our confidence therein. The dossier then encapsulates two or more linkage bundles, again with conclusions, rationale and confidence. Although we do not provide any pertinent examples in this volume, more complicated genealogical problems can lead to even higher levels, with two or more dossiers included in a more comprehensive dossier.

Note that this dossier also includes information that adds much to the genealogical definition of Hannah. We have learned that she had at least two spouses. The will of Abraham Tyler gives no indication that he had any children with Hannah (nor has any other record been found that indicates that this couple might have had children). If we assume that

Dossier: Hannah Farnham

Hannah Farnham no. 1
see page 84

....

....

Conclusion ....

Rationale ....

Confidence ....

Hannah Farnham no. 2
see page 85

....

....

Conclusion ....

Rationale ....

Confidence ....

Conclusion: A woman named Hannah Farnham married Abraham Tyler in 1650 and by 1673 was his widow. By 1695 this same woman had married Edward Brumidge and by 1700/1 was his widow. We have therefore traced the life of this one woman for half a century, from 1650 to 1700/1, and identified two husbands for her.

Rationale: The critical piece of evidence for this conclusion is the statement in the deed of 28 September 1695, in which the grantor calls herself "Hannah Brumidge of Haverhill ... formerly the wife of Abraham Tiler being his relict widow." We appeal again to the conclusion we reached earlier, that there was only one man by the name of Abraham Tyler in Haverhill, or indeed in Essex County, in the seventeenth century. On this basis, a woman claiming in 1695 to be the widow of Abraham Tyler would be identical with a woman making the same claim in 1673. We have no evidence of this woman between 1673 and 1695. She may have been widow for much of that time, or she may have married Edward Brumidge much earlier than 1695, or she may even have had another husband in the interim, as yet unidentified.

Confidence: Highly probable.

Figure 7.3.

Hannah was about 20 years old in 1650 at the time of her first marriage, then she would have been at least in her early forties by the time of her marriage to Edward Brumige, and perhaps older, so the chances are slim that she had any children with him, and certainly no other evidence has been found to suggest children by this marriage. Thus, although some uncertainty remains, and although we don't know what happened to Hannah after 1701, we have probably completed work on the part of Hannah's genealogical definition pertaining to spouses and children.

Now we return to our original question: What does this dossier for Hannah tell us about her parents? The immediate answer is "not much." If we assume that she was a young unmarried woman at the time of her first marriage, and married at the usual age of about 20 years, then she would have been born about 1630, give or take a few years. (A survey of all known Farnham and Varnum families in early New England does not reveal any male of that surname who had died by 1650 leaving a wife Hannah, supporting the assumption that Hannah Farnham had not been previously married before her marriage to Abraham Tyler.)

With this meager crop of information in hand, we now cast about for a Farnham family into which Hannah could have been born, probably about 1630. The first candidate family is that of Ralph Farnham, who came to New England in 1635 and settled at Ipswich.[3] He brought with him wife Alice, aged 28, and children Mary, aged 7; Thomas, aged 4; and Ralph, aged 2. Ralph Farnham did not generate many records in New England, but the evidence shows that he must have died by 1648, for on 18 June 1648 Solomon Martin married at Gloucester "Ales Varnam, widow, of Ipswich." The family then moved to Andover, Massachusetts, where several of the children of Ralph Farnham married in the 1650s and 1660s.

Andover is immediately adjacent to Haverhill, and both towns were a few miles to the northwest of Ipswich. Thus, if Hannah were a daughter of Ralph Farnham, a marriage in Haverhill would be quite reasonable. However, chronology argues against placing Hannah in the family of Ralph Farnham. As noted, when Ralph came to New England he had three children: Mary, Thomas, and Ralph. The ages given in the ship's passenger list for these children have been corroborated by baptisms in the parish of St. Nicholas, Rochester, Kent, which match precisely. As noted earlier, Hannah Farnham, wife of Abraham Tyler, was probably born about 1630, so, if she were a daughter of Ralph Farnham, her baptism should also have appeared in the Rochester church records and she should also have been on the 1635 passenger list. We could certainly postulate omissions and defects in these two records, but doing so would be piling unlikely hypothesis on unlikely hypothesis. Alternatively, Hannah could have been born after arrival in New England, but she would have been 15 years old or younger at the time of marriage to Abraham Tyler— not outside the range of possibility, but highly unusual at this time and place. We therefore conclude that the chances that Hannah (Farnham) (Tyler) Brumidge was daughter of Ralph Farnham are highly unlikely. In other words, we are unable to combine the dossier we have already created for Hannah Farnham with any linkage dossier we might create based on the family of Ralph Farnham to create an acceptable higher-level dossier which would claim that all the evidence contained in these two proposed dossiers pertains to the same family.

Note that Ralph Farnham's widow, Alice, at her remarriage, was called "Ales Varnam." Also, in the Ipswich town records, on 11 January

1640[/1], "Ralph Varneham" was paid for ringing the bell and cleaning the meetinghouse. And Thomas, son of Ralph, was on 2 April 1657 called "Thomas Varnham."[4]

Given this slight variability in the spelling of the surname, we note that a George Varnum had settled in Ipswich by 1635. In his will, dated 21 April 1649 and proved on an unknown date, "George Varnam of Ipswich" bequeathed "my house and barn & lands and goods and chattels to my wife for her life, and after her decease two parts of all my estate to my son Samuell Varnam and the third part to my daughter Hannah to be equally divided. And my meaning is if my son die without issue, my whole estate is to return to my daughter Hannah, and further so long as she remain unmarried is to enjoy a chamber in my house; and I do appoint Thomas Scott and my son Samuell to be my executors."[5]

Within the context of the family of George Varnum, these two mentions of Hannah in the will of the immigrant are all that we hear of this daughter. Even so, we can deduce a bit more about this woman. She had one sibling, brother Samuel, who deposed on 30 March 1668 "aged about forty-nine years,"[6] and so was born about 1619. The phrase "so long as she remain unmarried" as applied to Hannah could be interpreted to mean that she was already of marriageable age in 1649, and so was at least 20 years old. A working hypothesis from these clues would be that Hannah Varnum was born sometime in the 1620s, perhaps toward the end of that decade.

We now have two partial lives, two dossiers: a Hannah Varnum born perhaps in the 1620s and alive and not yet married in 1649; and a Hannah Farnham who married for the first time in 1650, married again in 1673, and was living in 1701. Note that the first of these two dossiers would be created by someone interested in the family of George Varnum, working from the past to the present. The second dossier would be generated by a hypothetical descendant of Abraham Tyler or Edward Brumidge, working from the present to the past. Can we merge these two dossiers to generate a complete life?

If we do choose to link these two partial lives, then we would be able to make the simple genealogical deduction that Hannah Farnham, wife of Abraham Tyler (and later of Edward Brumidge), was the daughter of George Varnum of Ipswich. The evidence shows that George Varnum did have a daughter Hannah, whereas Ralph Farnham probably did not. The chronological fit is good, and Haverhill is close to Ipswich. But that is not sufficient. No other bits of circumstantial evidence connect Abraham Tyler to any other member of the family of George Varnum. Although the chances are slim, Ralph Farnham *could* have had a daughter Hannah who married Abraham Tyler at a relatively young age.

In the absence of further evidence, therefore, we judge that the identification of Hannah, daughter of George Varnum, as the wife of Abraham Tyler, is somewhere on the boundary between highly possible and barely probable. More relevant data would be welcome.[7]

Example Two: Three Jacob Dearborns, with different levels of confidence

Again we present a diagram (Figure 7.4) to set the parameters of the problem. In this example there is a partial pedigree with three first cousins by the name of Jacob Dearborn, grandsons of Jacob[4] Dearborn. All three were born within the space of a few years, all within a relatively constrained portion of the southern coast of Maine.

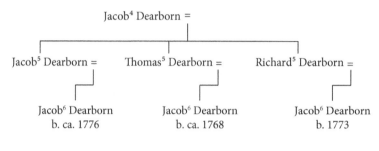

Figure 7.4.

We then have three additional partial pedigrees, in which three men by the name of Jacob Dearborn were married in the same part of Maine, also in a narrow time frame.[8] (See Figure 7.5.)

1790			1797			1806	
Jacob	=	Olive	Jacob	=	Hannah	Jacob	=	Hannah
Dearborn		Stone	Dearborn		Rookes	Dearborn		Whitney

Figure 7.5.

How do we connect these partial Dearborn family networks? How do we tie together some of the loose threads dangling off these incomplete tapestries?

Two points are relevant here. First, as noted when discussing points of comparison (see page 37), similarity of name is not enough evidence upon which to base an identification. This may seem excruciatingly obvious, but it is one of the commonest of genealogical mistakes among beginners. In the present instance, the narrow ranges of time and locations of the births of three Jacobs and the marriages of three Jacobs makes such a facile identification especially dangerous.

Second, a more mechanical point: the importance of drawing diagrams of each problem you consider must be reemphasized. The simple act of putting what you know on paper, with the minimum of dates, forces you to confront problems of chronology, and of confused generations.

Linkage Bundle: Jacob Dearborn no. 1

On 4 May 1797, Jacob Dearborn and Hannah Rooks were married at Orrington, Maine.

On 22 June 1847, Jacob Dearborn of Cincinnati, Ohio, stated that "my father he was born in September 1743, his name was Richard Dearborn. . . . I Jacob Dearborn was married to my wife Hannah Rookes in June 20 1797."

Conclusion: The Jacob Dearborn who married Hannah Rooks at Orrington, Maine, in 1797 was son of Richard Dearborn.

Rationale: The conclusion derives directly from the statement made by Jacob Dearborn in the second of these records. However, two chronological discrepancies require attention:
1. Jacob stated that his father Richard was born in September 1743, whereas the Richard Dearborn in question was known to have been baptized between 26 August 1747 and 13 September 1747. Thus, the month is probably correct, but not the year. Elsewhere in the letter, Jacob stated that he is replying "as far as my memory permits," suggesting that he is not relying on written records. Furthermore, he names a number of his brothers, which can be matched with other data for this Richard.
2. Jacob said that he was married on 20 June 1797, whereas the marriage record is for 4 May 1797. This again is probably a defect of memory; otherwise we would have to postulate two men named Jacob Dearborn both marrying women named Hannah Rooks in Orrington within two months of one another, for which there is no evidence. (Another letter in the collection, from Jacob's son Jacob, stated that the family had resided in Orrington.)

Confidence: Almost certain.

Figure 7.6.

One of these Jacobs himself provided one of the desired connections. Edmund B. Dearborn, a distant cousin of David Dearborn, was also reference librarian at NEHGS, from 1846 to 1849. A century and a half ago he compiled a substantial manuscript genealogy of the Dearborn family, which provided a beginning point for much of David's work. In Edmund Dearborn's files is a letter from a Jacob Dearborn, dated Cincinnati, Ohio, on 22 June 1847, which states:

> my father he was born in September 1743, his name was Richard Dearborn and my father died in January about 27 years ago. . . . I Jacob Dearborn was married to my wife Hannah Rookes in June 20 1797.

This information meshes well with the known data. In effect, the correspondent Jacob Dearborn has created the linkage bundle for us. Jacob Dearborn, son of Richard, was born in 1773, and so would have been about 24 years old at his marriage to Hannah Rookes, an appropriate age for that time and place (See Figure 7.6.). This leaves us with two Jacob births to match up with two Jacob marriages.

Linkage Bundle: Jacob Dearborn no. 2

On 14 April 1806, Jacob Dearborn of Township Two and Hannah Whitney of Hampden were married at Hampden, Maine.

Jacob and Hannah Dearborn named their twelfth and last child Elias.

A nineteenth-century source stated that Jacob Dearborn of the fifth generation had a son named Jacob.

Conclusion: The Jacob Dearborn who married Hannah Whitney at Hampden, Maine, in 1806 was son of Jacob Dearborn.

Rationale: The principal evidence tying these three records together is the rarity of the given name Elias. A Jacob Dearborn of the fifth generation was known to have had a son Elias and probably had a son Jacob. The Jacob Dearborn who married Hannah Whitney named a son Elias and was of the right age to be son of the fifth generation Jacob. Thus, the Jacob Dearborn who married Hannah Whitney fits very nicely as son of Jacob Dearborn of the fifth generation.

Confidence: Highly probable.

Figure 7.7.

David then observed that the Jacob Dearborn who married Hannah Whitney at Hampden, Maine, in 1806, was described in his marriage record as a resident of Township 2. In 1819 this township was named Newburgh, where this Jacob remained until his death in 1860. Jacob and Hannah (Whitney) Dearborn had twelve children, the last of whom was Elias Dearborn, born in July 1831. Elias was a very rare given name in the Dearborn family, but Jacob[6] Dearborn, son of Jacob[5], had a brother Elias.

On this strong piece of circumstantial evidence, David concluded that the parentage of Jacob of Newburgh had been satisfactorily established. Note that no contemporaneous record shows *directly* that Jacob[5] had a son named Jacob. Prior to David's analysis, this claim was based solely on a late nineteenth-century secondary source. Jacob Dearborn of Newburgh, Maine, was aged 74 in the 1850 census and 84 at his death in 1860. This would place his birth in about 1776, which would make him the eldest child of Jacob[5] Dearborn with his second wife, Hannah Martin, in agreement with his placement in that secondary source. (See Figure 7.7.)

Linkage Bundle: Jacob Dearborn no. 3

On 6 July 1790, Jacob Dearborn and Olive Stone were married at Scarborough, Maine.

On 13 November 1768, Jacob Dearborn, son of Thomas Dearborn, was baptized at Pepperellborough [Saco], Maine.

On 18 April 1793, Thomas Dearborn, son of Jacob Dearborn, was born at Pepperellborough.

Conclusion: The Jacob Dearborn who married Olive Stone at Scarborough, Maine, in 1790 was son of Thomas Dearborn.

Rationale: Three lines of circumstantial evidence tie these three records together:
1. 1790 would be an appropriate date for the first marriage of a man born in 1768.
2. The Jacob Dearborn who married Olive Stone resided in the same town in which the Jacob Dearborn, son of Thomas, was baptized.
3. The son Thomas born to Jacob Dearborn in 1793 could have been named for Jacob's father.

Confidence: Probable.

Figure 7.8.

We are now left with Jacob Dearborn, baptized in 1768, son of Thomas, and with the Jacob Dearborn who married Olive Stone at Scarborough, Maine, in 1790. This latter Jacob named a son Thomas, which would be appropriate if he was himself son of a Thomas. And Jacob, son of Thomas, would have been 22 years old at the time of the marriage of a Jacob to Olive Stone. On this basis, David concluded that Jacob[6] (*Thomas*[5]) Dearborn was the man who married Olive Stone. (See Figure 7.8.)

We might entertain the possibility that this latter marriage was made by some other Jacob Dearborn, from another branch of the Dearborn family, who had wandered into the territory of the descendants of Jacob[4] Dearborn. After forty years of research on this family, however, David Dearborn has not found another Jacob of the right age in any other branch.

As satisfying as this solution is, the strengths of the conclusions reached are not the same for each of these three Jacobs. If we accept the validity and the accuracy of the 1847 letter of Jacob Dearborn naming his father as Richard and his wife as Hannah Rooks, we conclude that this identification is about as strong as a genealogical conclusion can be and may be classified as *almost certain*.

The identification of Jacob[6] (*Jacob*[5]) as the one who married Hannah Whitney, based as it is on the use of an uncommon given name, and to a lesser extent on a good chronological fit, may be classified as not quite as strong, perhaps at the level of *highly probable*.

Finally, the evidence tying Jacob[6] (*Thomas*[5]) to the marriage with Olive Stone is perhaps one step less probable, since the use of the name Thomas for a son does not have the same evidentiary strength as does the use of the name Elias in the previous instance. We may assign this piece of linkage analysis a level of *probable*.

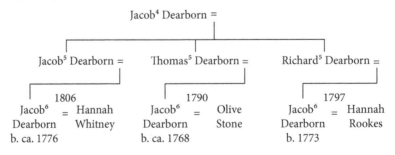

Figure 7.9.

Figure 7.9 shows the single, larger pedigree derived from the four partial pedigrees with which we started.

▧ **John Borden** *(cont. from Chapter Three)*

In Chapter Three we gathered four records for a John Borden who lived in Watertown between 1652 and 1658, connected them in a single linkage bundle, and concluded that all four records pertained to a single individual, probably born in the mid-1630s. This linkage bundle would be of interest to anyone studying the family of a John Borden who appeared at New London, Connecticut, in the early 1660s; such a researcher, looking for the origin of John Borden of New London, might wonder whether John Borden of Watertown could provide that earlier history.

We will not at this point go through the arguments linking all the records for John Borden of Connecticut, but let's assume that we have created a large linkage bundle for this man. So we will select for our immediate purposes just those two records which bear on the question of whether John Borden of Connecticut is identical with the John Borden who was in Watertown from 1652 to 1658.

The two pertinent items from John Borden of Connecticut's linkage bundle are the following:

> John Borden and Hannah Hough were married at New London on 11 July 1661.[9]

> John Borden was admitted to the town privileges at New London in January 1661/2.[10]

The second item, the admission to town privileges, implies that this John Borden was 21 years old by January 1661/2, which further implies that he must have been born no later than January 1640/1. The first item, the marriage record, suggests that the John Borden who married Hannah Hough was a few years older; most New England men at this point in the seventeenth century made their first marriage at about 25 years of age. That would place the year of birth of John Borden of New London at about 1636. These are the only two records from this linkage bundle that bear upon the date of birth of this man.

From this linkage bundle, therefore, we are able to arrive at the substantive conclusion that a man named John Borden, born probably in the mid-1630s and not known to be previously married, arrived in New London, Connecticut, no later than the summer of 1661. (In reaching this substantive conclusion, we made use of two items of specific external knowledge: in early New England, most men married for the first time at about 25 years of age; and in colonial New England the age for being accepted as an inhabitant of a town with full privileges was 21.) See Figure 7.10.

> ### Linkage Bundle: John Borden no. 2
>
> On 11 July 1661, John Borden and Hannah Hough were married at New London, Connecticut.
>
> In January 1661/2, John Borden was admitted to town privileges at New London.
>
> On 5 August 1677, Joanna Borden, daughter of John and Hannah, was born at New London.
>
> **Conclusion:** A man named John Borden, born no later than 1641 and perhaps about 1636, had arrived at New London, Connecticut, by 1661.
>
> **Rationale:** There are many more records for the name John Borden at New London, but the first two of the records above are the earliest, and are most directly relevant to the problem under study. Both events recorded in these two items are appropriate for a man just attaining adulthood. Nothing in these two records (or in any of the other records for a John Borden in the immediately following years) indicates that there was more than one John Borden in New London at this time, so we may conclude that these two records pertain to the same man.
>
> In order to be admitted to town privileges, a man must have been at least 21, so this John Borden would have been born in 1641 or earlier. At this time in colonial New England, men generally made their first marriage at about the age of 25, so this John Borden would likely have been born about 1636.
>
> The third record here clearly belongs to the same family and will be employed at a later stage in our argument.
>
> **Confidence:** Highly probable.

Figure 7.10.

Comparing the Watertown linkage bundle with the New London linkage bundle for men named John Borden, we can say at most that nothing would prevent these two sets of records from pertaining to the same man. Both linkage bundles describe men born in the mid-1630s, and there are no chronological conflicts between the two sets of records. So, our tentative conclusion is that these two linkage bundles could refer to the same man. This conclusion is far from proved, however; we need further evidence. Casting about for the name John Borden in other New England records, we notice that the name also appears in records from Dedham, Massachusetts, a town close to Watertown.

Although not immediately obvious (given the odd spellings of the surname), the following items from the early church and vital records of Dedham will be found to be relevant:

1635 John, the son of John Balden and Joana his wife, was borne the 24th of the 4th month[11]

1639 Samuell, the son of John & Joanna Gay, was borne the 10 of the 1 month[12]

_____ Gay the wife of John Gay was received with good satisfaction to the church the 25 of the 5 month [July] [1639][13]

John Balducke the son of our sister Gay by her first husband was baptized the 8th day of the 6 month 1639

Samuel Gay son of our sister Gay by her 2d husband was baptized the same day[14]

The final pair of records, which appear sequentially in the Dedham church register, demonstrate that "sister Gay" was married twice, first to a man with the surname "Balducke" and then to a man named "Gay." We will condense the chain of reasoning somewhat by stipulating that the second husband was John Gay, early settler of Watertown and then Dedham, that the name of his only known wife was Joanna, and that she is the woman admitted to Dedham church on 5 July 1639.

What can be made of the unusual surname Balducke? This spelling appears nowhere else in early Dedham records, and it has been rendered in even stranger forms in the secondary literature. At this point, we recall our discussion in Chapter One of Reverend John Allin of Dedham and his difficulty with names and postulate that "Balducke" was somehow generated by Allin's pen as a distortion of some other surname. When we survey other Dedham records, the closest approximation we find is the birth record for "John Balden" on 24 June 1635. The name of this child's mother was Joanna, the same name as the mother of "John Balducke," the woman who married John Gay as her second husband. This 1635 birth record marks the only mention of the surname Balden in early Dedham records. It seems safe to propose, then, that all of the records collected just above constitute a single linkage bundle (Figure 7.11), built around a woman whom we shall designate as Joanna (_____) (Balden) Gay, wife successively of John Balden and John Gay.

The next step is to examine further the family of John Gay in hopes of finding more evidence about Joanna's first husband and his family. Two items stand out from others:

First, the second son of John and Joanna Gay was a son Hezekiah, born at Dedham on 3 July 1640. This young man died at Dedham on 28 November 1669, unmarried and leaving behind a nuncupative (oral) will, in which he named his Gay siblings, but also included a bequest of clothing to "my brother John Bord . . . I think he have most need, they are hardest to be gotten there."[15] Is "Bord" another version of "Balden" and "Balducke"? One possibility is that "Bord" is an abbreviated form of "Borden," and that "Borden" and "Balden" are simple variants of a common surname, with

Linkage Bundle: John Borden no. 3

On 24 June 1635, "John, the son of John Balden and Joana his wife," was born at Dedham, Massachusetts.

On 10 May 1638/9, "Samuel, the son of John & Joanna Gay," was born at Dedham.

On 25 July 1639, "_____ Gay the wife of John Gay was received with good satisfaction to the church" at Dedham.

On 8 August 1639, "John Balducke the son of our sister Gay by her first husband" was baptized at Dedham. "Samuel Gay son of our sister Gay by her 2d husband was baptized the same day."

On 25 October 1669, "Hezekiah Gay the son of John Gay of Dedham" bequeathed to "my brother John Bord [clothing], I think he have most need, they are hardest to be gotten there."

On 1 March 1689/90, "Johanna Gay, widow, the relict of John Gay Senior," bequeathed to "my loving grandchild Joanna Borden."

Conclusion: A child named John Balden was born at Dedham, Massachusetts, on 24 June 1635 and was baptized there on 8 August 1639. His mother, Joanna, had married John Gay as her second husband. John Balden and Samuel Gay were, therefore, half-brothers.

Rationale: The fourth item, a single entry in the church records that documents two baptisms, demonstrates that the mother of "John Balducke" and "Samuel Gay" had married twice, to a man named "Balducke" and then to a man named "Gay." This woman had been admitted as a member of Dedham church just two weeks before these two baptisms. The birth record for Samuel Gay shows that her given name was Joanna and her second husband was John Gay. (Many later records for John Gay show that his only wife over a period of five decades was named Joanna.)

The 1635 birth record for John Balden may be linked to the 1639 baptism of John Balducke if we can reconcile the difference in surname. This is accomplished by observing that Reverend John Allin, who maintained the Dedham church records at the time, was notoriously bad with names, and the supposed surname "Balducke" appears nowhere else. Thus, we conclude with substantial assurance that the 1635 birth record for John Balden and the 1639 baptism for John Balducke pertain to the same individual.

The final two records clearly pertain to the John and Joanna Gay of the previous records, and will be used at a later stage of our argument.

Confidence: Highly probable.

Figure 7.11.

"Balducke" as Reverend Allin's personal aberration. At this point we must undertake some record analysis in hopes of resolving this issue. The most readily available version of Hezekiah Gay's will is in the nineteenth-century copy of the seventeenth-century register of Suffolk County wills. Given the orthographical practices of the period, it is not difficult to imagine that the nineteenth-century clerk simply misread the name, or that the seventeenth-century scribe had rendered the name as Bord', the apostrophe a sort of terminal flourish indicating that the surname was being abbreviated. Fortunately, the seventeenth-century version of the probate register survives and is available. An examination determines that the surname was entered there as Bord, without a terminal flourish. The next logical step would be to examine the probate file, which should have the version of the will which was used to create the register copy. Unfortunately, no file exists for this probate case, and so the trail of evidence ends.

Second, in her will of 1 March 1689/90, Joanna Gay, widow of John Gay, includes a bequest to "my loving grandchild Joanna Borden." This grandchild was not a child of any of the sons and daughters that Joanna had with her second husband, John Gay. At this point, we can conclude that Borden is the surname hinted at by the variations of Balducke, Balden, and Bord, and that a better designation for the testatrix, and the center of this linkage bundle, is Joanna (_____) (Borden) Gay.

We are now in a position to go back to the two linkage bundles that we created earlier, from Watertown and New London records, and make another attempt to tie them together. First, among the children of John and Hannah (Hough) Borden of New London and Lyme was a daughter Joanna, born on 5 August 1677. No other woman of this name of the right age to be a grandchild of Joanna (_____) (Borden) Gay has been found in early New England. Second, Watertown and Dedham are adjacent towns, and John Gay had resided briefly at Watertown prior to his settlement at Dedham. Third, the statement by Hezekiah Gay, with relation to "my brother John Bord," that clothing is "hardest to be gotten there," suggests that this brother lived in a community not close to a major trading town, which would describe Lyme, Connecticut, at that time.

Taken all together, the claim that all three John Borden linkage bundles, based in Dedham, Watertown, and Connecticut, pertain to the same individual is reasonable and well supported, reaching the confidence level of highly probable. John Borden, son of John and Joanna Borden, born in 1635, was soon orphaned by the death of his father, was taken in to the family of John Gay of Dedham through the remarriage of his mother, and by the early 1650s was apprenticed to Charles Chadwick of the neighboring town of Watertown. Then, a few years after the conclusion of his apprenticeship, he moved to New London, Connecticut, where he married and raised a large family. The dossier we have created for John Borden is shown in Figure 7.12.

Dossier: John Borden

John Borden no. 1 see page 53	John Borden no. 2 see page 96	John Borden no. 3 see page 98
. . . .	. . . .	. . . .
. . . .	. . . .	. . . .
Conclusion	Conclusion	Conclusion . . . .
Rationale	Rationale	Rationale . . . .
Confidence	Confidence	Confidence . . . .

Conclusion: John Borden was born at Dedham, Massachusetts, on 24 June 1635 and was baptized there on 8 August 1639, son of John and Joanna Borden. From 1652 to 1658 he resided at Watertown, Massachusetts, as apprentice to Charles Chadwick. By 1661 he had moved to New London, Connecticut, where he married Hannah Hough and was admitted to the town privileges.

Rationale: First, we compare the second linkage bundle with the third, taking special note of the fifth and sixth records in the third linkage bundle. Hezekiah Gay leaves a bequest of clothing to "John Bord," with the comment that "they are hardest to be gotten there," implying that "John Bord" lived at some distance from Dedham, in a town distant from trading centers. Since we don't have a contemporary copy of Hezekiah's will, we observe that "Bord" could well have been intended for "Borden."

Joanna Gay, widow of John Gay (and mother of Hezekiah Gay), left a bequest to "my loving grandchild Joanna Borden." Borden was a rare surname at this time in New England, and the only available Joanna Borden was the daughter of John and Hannah Borden of New London and Lyme. We conclude, then, that John Borden of New London was the same individual as John Balden, born at Dedham in 1635, son of John and Joanna Balden (or Borden), stepson of John Gay, and halfbrother of Hezekiah Gay.

With this conclusion in hand, we note that Dedham and Watertown were adjacent to one another and that John Gay had resided briefly at Watertown prior to his move to Dedham. Thus, the records for a John Borden at Watertown from 1652 to 1658 fit well with what we know of John Borden of Dedham and Watertown and describe an appropriate episode in his life.

Confidence: Highly probable.

Figure 7.12.

Thus, through the construction of three linkage bundles, and the amalgamation of these three constructs into one dossier, we have delineated a full life, including a number of migrations. We have woven together two incomplete tapestries and settled two reciprocal points of genealogical definition: John Borden, son of John and Joanna Borden, married Hannah Hough; and John Borden, the husband of Hannah Hough, was the son of John and Joanna Borden.[16]

Rachel Hart *(cont. from Chapter Three)*

In Chapter Two we introduced a single record from the Winthrop Medical Journal for a woman named Rachel Hart. In Chapter Three we added to this single record four more for the same name from the same source, and then linked those five records into a single bundle pertaining to one woman named Rachel Hart.

At the end of the discussion of Rachel Hart in Chapter Three, we also pointed out the serendipitous discovery of a record for a Stephen Hart, stated to be brother of Rachel. Examination of Savage's *Genealogical Dictionary of New England* and other secondary sources shows that there was a Stephen Hart who first settled in Cambridge, Massachusetts, by 1632, then moved on to Hartford and finally Farmington in Connecticut.[17] This Stephen Hart had a son Stephen who would have been about the right age to be brother of Rachel, but Savage and other sources make no mention of Rachel.

In his will, the elder Stephen Hart included bequests to "my beloved daughters Sarah Porter, Marie Lee and my son-in-law John Cole."[18] Various secondary sources state that the wife of John Cole was Mehitable Hart, daughter of Stephen,[19] but nothing found in the contemporary records for the family of Stephen Hart mentions a daughter Mehitable.

At this point, another search was made in the Winthrop Medical Journal for the name John Cole. Ten entries were found for a woman named Rachel Cole, several of which give her husband as John Cole. From these ten records we will create a second linkage bundle.[20]

> 12 December 1664: Cole John his wife Rachell *male fluebant menses* [poor menstrual flow] . . .
>
> 25 November 1665: Cole John his wife Rachell . . . [various maladies including] hath now pain in head . . . [prescribed medication] for her eyes . . .
>
> 24 December 1665: Cole John his wife Rachell vide Nov. 25 1665 . . . much head pain . . .
>
> 14 February 1665/6: Cole Rachel wife of John of Hartford . . . [various treatments then on 22 February] fainted in the morning & sight gone a while . . .
>
> 31 March 1666: Cole Rachel vide 14 February . . .

18 April 1666: Cole Rachell wife of John Cole of Hartford vide formerly Mar: 31 . . .

21 May 1666: Cole Rachell vide formerly Apr: 18 1666 . . .

7 July 1666: Cole Rachell vide formerly May 21 1666 . . .

18 May 1667: Cole Rachell wife of John Cole of Farmington vide 7 July 1666 . . . advised to shrink up her eyes . . .

4 May 1669: Cole Rachell wife of [blank] Cole of Farmington . . . dim eyes . . .

As with the earlier group of records for Rachel Hart, internal cross-references explicitly link several of these entries. The phrase "vide Nov. 25 1665" is an instruction to look back at the entry for this same name on 25 November 1665, the word *vide* being Latin for "see." Thus, the third item refers to the second. The next six items, the fourth through the ninth, are likewise chained together into one group by a series of back-references. On the basis of this feature alone, we are able to consolidate these ten entries into four bundles: item one; items two and three; items four through nine; and item ten.

Examination of the medical substance of these entries allows us to take the next step, combining three of these four bundles into a larger bundle comprising nine of the ten entries. Rachel Cole suffered from a variety of maladies, but a recurring theme is a problem with her eyes: medication "for her eyes" [25 November 1665]; "sight gone a while" [14 February 1665/6]; "advised to shrink up her eyes" [18 May 1667]; and "dim eyes" [4 May 1669].

At this point, only one of the entries, the first, remains unlinked. To connect this item to the other nine, we observe that a survey of the standard New England secondary sources reveals only two other men by the name of John Cole in New England at this time: John Cole of Hartford, whose only known wife was Mary (and who was father of the husband of Rachel); and John Cole of Milford, whose wife's given name is not known. Thus, there appears to have been only one John Cole in Connecticut (and indeed in all of New England) with a wife named Rachel. Although the argument for linking the first of these ten entries to the other nine is perhaps not as strong as linking the second through tenth items, the likelihood that all ten of these records pertain to the same woman is very high, and we proceed on that basis. (Figure 7.13 shows the relevant linkage bundle.)

What more can we extract from this bundle of records, now that they have been linked? First, although not directly relevant to the problem we are attempting to solve, we may conclude that this John Cole and his family moved from Hartford to Farmington sometime between 18 April 1666 and 18 May 1667.

Linkage Bundle: Rachel Hart no. 2

12 December 1664: Cole John his wife Rachell *male fluebant menses*.

25 November 1665: Cole John his wife Rachell . . . for her eyes.

24 December 1665: Cole John his wife Rachell vide Nov. 25 1665.

14 February 1665/6: Cole Rachel wife of John of Hartford . . . sight gone awhile.

31 March 1666: Cole Rachel vide 14 February.

18 April 1666: Cole Rachell wife of John Cole of Hartford vide formerly Mar: 31.

21 May 1666: Cole Rachell vide formerly Apr: 18 1666.

7 July 1666: Cole Rachell vide formerly May 21 1666.

18 May 1667: Cole Rachell wife of John Cole of Farmington vide 7 July 1666 . . . advised to shrink up her eyes.

4 May 1669: Cole Rachell wife of [blank] Cole of Farmington . . . dim eyes.

Conclusion: Between 1664 a man named John Cole had a wife Rachel. In late 1666 or early 1667, this couple moved from Hartford to Farmington.

Rationale: Internal cross-references help link these ten records. The third record refers to the second, thus strongly linking these two records. The fourth through ninth records are likewise firmly joined by a similar but longer sequence of such back-references.

As a second step we note the common diagnosis of problems with the eyes, mentioned in entries two, four, nine and ten. Combining this point of comparison with the back-references, we conclude that the second through the ninth of these records pertain to the same individual. Only the first record is unconnected.

We do have *negative* evidence: no known evidence indicates the existence of another John Cole with wife Rachel at this date, and there is no inconsistency in including the first record with the other nine. With the decision that these ten records pertain to the same individual, the deduction of the move from Hartford to Farmington flows naturally.

Confidence: Highly probable.

Figure 7.13.

Second, we observe that, uncharacteristically, in none of these ten records does John Winthrop Jr. state the age of the patient. This is disappointing. When this John Cole made his will on 12 September 1689, he left wife Rachel and five children, the eldest of whom was a son John, aged 24 and therefore born about 1665.[21] Thus, John Cole and Rachel were probably recently married at the time of her visit with John Winthrop Jr. on 12 December 1664.

The question now is whether this bundle of ten records for Rachel Cole can be linked with the earlier bundle for Rachel Hart, to create a dossier that begins to encompass the entire life of one woman. Such a linkage is certainly possible. Within the limits of what we have gleaned only from the Winthrop Medical Journal, we know that Rachel Hart and Rachel Cole were about the same age, both resided in Hartford, and both suffered from eye problems. This is promising, but not sufficient. There may have been more than one woman of this generation in Hartford named Rachel. We need more evidence before we can reach a conclusion that is any greater than possible.

For this additional evidence we return to the serendipitous discovery of the Winthrop Medical Journal record for Stephen Hart, and the further information we generated above about this man's family. The adjacency of the two records on 21 November 1657 in the Winthrop Medical Journal provides the only evidence that the immigrant Stephen Hart had a daughter Rachel. The will of Stephen Hart shows that he had a daughter who married a man named John Cole. As noted above, there were not many men by the name of John Cole in early Connecticut, and only one had a wife Rachel. We are now justified in rejecting the existence of a Mehitable Hart and declaring that the two linkage bundles derived from the Winthrop Medical Journal *do* pertain to the same individual, with a confidence level of highly probable. (See Figure 7.14.) Again, we have simultaneously solved two reciprocal problems: Stephen Hart's daughter Rachel married John Cole; John Cole's wife was Rachel Hart, daughter of Stephen.

Two further points may be made. First, the claim made about the existence of only one John Cole in Connecticut at this time with a wife named Rachel derives much of its strength from the principle of record density. The number of records available for Connecticut in the seventeenth century, and especially for Hartford and Farmington, is sufficient for us to make this claim with a high degree of confidence. We might not be able to do so in a place and time characterized by low record density.

Second, further searching in the secondary literature shows that John and Rachel Cole had a son John who married in the early 1690s Mehitable Loomis. Some earlier researcher, unable to find a marriage record for a

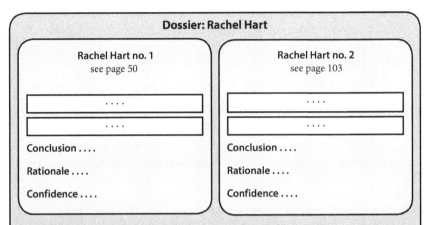

Dossier: Rachel Hart

Rachel Hart no. 1	Rachel Hart no. 2
see page 50	see page 103
. . . .	. . . .
. . . .	. . . .
Conclusion	Conclusion . . . .
Rationale	Rationale . . . .
Confidence	Confidence . . . .

Conclusion: Between 1659 and 1664, Rachel Hart, born about 1642, daughter of Stephen Hart of Hartford, married John Cole of Hartford.

Rationale: Examined in isolation, these two linkage bundles are consistent with one another and could reasonably pertain to the same person. In the 1650s we see a young unmarried woman named Rachel with eye problems residing in Hartford. Then, in the 1660s we see a married woman named Rachel with eye problems residing in Hartford. This observation is not sufficient to link these two bundles of records with any high degree of confidence.

One of the records for Rachel Hart was adjacent to a record for her brother Stephen Hart, known to be son of the immigrant Stephen Hart. In his will of 16 March 1682/3, the immigrant Stephen Hart included a bequest to "my son-in-law John Cole." Combining this with the observation that there was no other John Cole in the vicinity at that time, we now have high confidence in linking these two bundles, and in extracting from the resulting dossier the conclusion stated above.

Confidence: Highly probable.

Figure 7.14.

daughter of Stephen Hart to a John Cole, must have latched onto this later marriage, and, despite the chronological impossibility, chosen to invent a Mehitable Hart. This case of misidentification by generation slippage is a common phenomenon.

(In 1995 Gale Ion Harris traced another woman from her youth to marriage by following her in the Winthrop Medical Journal. Sarah Risley, daughter of Richard Risley, was born about 1640 and was "between 7 and 8 years old" when her father died about 1648. She is found, as Sarah Risley, in entries in the Winthrop Medical Journal dated in 1658 and 1660. Then in 1668 Sarah Crooke, wife of Samuel Crooke, was treated by John Winthrop Jr. Harris notes that her "given name, residence, and affliction together suggest that she may be the same person" as Sarah Risley. He then proceeds to marshal additional circumstantial evidence in support of this hypothesis.[22])

Summary

In this chapter we have employed the technique of linkage analysis at a higher level than was done in Chapter Three. We have taken existing linkage bundles and attempted to combine them together into larger constructs, or **dossiers,** in each case providing a **rationale** for our conclusions. In the Farnham example, no firm conclusion was reached, although this does not mean that no progress was made. In the Jacob Dearborn example, we were able to reach a reasonable set of conclusions, albeit at different levels of confidence. In the Borden and Hart case studies we obtained conclusions that may be labeled highly probable. In Chapter Eight we will examine more closely the criteria by which we have determined that we have resolved a given problem.

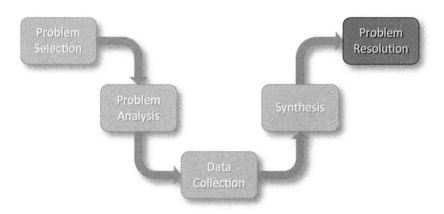

Chapter Eight

Problem Resolution

As we have emphasized throughout this book, the solution of a genealogical problem is always the result of the joining of two or more linkage bundles or dossiers. Merging two or more bundles into a dossier, however, does not always lead to the satisfactory solution of a genealogical problem, as shown in the case of Hannah Farnham in the last chapter.

In this chapter we will review the final stages of some of the problems discussed in early chapters, to clarify just what constitutes **problem resolution**. Two additional case studies will further exemplify these criteria, and the chapter will conclude with a brief discussion of a final strategy that may assist us in problem resolution.

Criteria of Problem Resolution

In Chapter Four, Problem Selection, we introduced the concept of **genealogical definition** of an individual: minimally connecting that individual to his or her parents, spouse (or spouses), and children (see page 58). Having now proceeded through a number of case studies, in some instances resolving a genealogical problem and in other instances not, let's return to the idea of genealogical definition and see how it relates to problem resolution.

In the case of Rachel Hart, the first step was to create a linkage bundle for a woman of that name, relying only on the records in the Winthrop Medical Journal. The next step was to create a second linkage bundle for a woman named Rachel Cole, again relying solely on the same source. These two sets of conjoined records, when considered in isolation, could not be confidently linked to one another. Only when we explored the connections of the first linkage bundle in another direction, using evidence from the records of Rachel Hart's father and brother, were we able to make a confident linkage and resolve the problem.

As for John Borden, the linkage bundles created for a John Borden of Watertown and a John Borden of New London had points of similarity, but again we could not weld them together with any confidence. Once we had brought in a third set of records, for a John Borden of Dedham, we were able to pull all three bundles into one larger dossier, and declare the genealogical problem to be solved.

Therefore we can make the following general observations:

- The resolution of a genealogical problem will always arise from a series of linkage decisions, that is, from serial application of the Second Fundamental Rule of Genealogy: You must have a sound, explicit reason for saying that any two individual records refer to the same person.

- Most of the linkage decisions a researcher makes do not directly address the genealogical problem of interest. Typical linkage decisions focus on determining whether two deeds refer to the same piece of land, or whether an individual holding a local office is the same as an individual of the same name who had been admitted to colony freemanship.

- As you build from linking individual records into a bundle, and then linking two or more bundles into a dossier, you will be recreating the life of a person. At some point, almost trivially, as the life of that person takes better shape, the resolution to the genealogical problem you are working on will gradually emerge.

- Directly comparing the process of record linkage with the concept of genealogical definition, we find that we never solve a single genealogical problem, but always two reciprocal problems. In demonstrating that the wife of John Cole was Rachel Hart, we have also shown that the daughter of Stephen Hart married John Cole. From the perspective of our imagery of unfinished tapestries, we have tied together the edges of two tapestries, finding that a loose thread in one is now connected to a loose thread in the other. We have resolved an unanswered question of genealogical definition in one incomplete pedigree by showing that it is the other end, the other half, of an unanswered question of genealogical definition in another incomplete pedigree.

- This last observation illuminates another aspect of problem resolution: *The solution to a genealogical problem may be possible when approached from one direction, but not from the other.* Sometimes a genealogist compiling a volume containing all the descendants of an immigrant will run into a dead end, such as an inability to determine the fate of a great-grandchild of the immigrant. Once the volume is published, a descendant will come forward with the crucial piece of evidence, which has been preserved only among the descendants of that great-grandchild. And the opposite situation can occur as well. A genealogist may be tracing his or her ancestry and come to a dead end some generations back. The answer may be found in records of a much earlier generation, provided by some other researcher studying all the early families of a given time and place. The bottom-up and the top-down approaches may *both* be necessary.

- The technique of linkage analysis, the full application of the Second Fundamental Rule, can resolve problems of genealogical importance in addition to those directly bearing on genealogical definition. First, as in the case of John Borden, these techniques may also allow us to follow migrations of individuals. By linking the records of John Borden of Dedham with those of John Borden of New London, we were able to settle a number of questions of genealogical definition. But by also including the records of John Borden of Watertown, it was possible to add to our biographical knowledge of this man's wanderings without directly adding to our genealogical knowledge of that man. Second, as shown later in this chapter, researchers are often confronted with the problem of carefully distinguishing two or more men of the same name, a problem that these same tools can help resolve.

Case Studies

Samuel Gay *(cont. from Chapter Four)*

In the discussion of problem selection in Chapter Four, we noted that the parentage of Abigail, only wife of Samuel Gay, was unknown, and that we needed this information for her to be fully defined. We do have some information about Abigail. We know her age at death, and we can calculate an approximate birth year. We in fact have much information about her life from 1688 until her death in 1744; what we are missing are the details of her life before 1688, which would obviously include her birth and her connection with her parents. This situation is one of the commonest that researchers encounter in genealogical work—we have a portion of an individual's life history and are casting about for the remainder of that life. In this case we are looking for the early years of a girl named Abigail, which we can unite with the later history that we already have, to form the complete picture of a life. We possess an incomplete weaving, one of the dangling threads being Abigail, wife of Samuel Gay.

As in the case of Hannah Farnham in Chapter Seven, we commence by building a linkage bundle based on Abigail's life as wife of Samuel Gay. In the case of Hannah Farnham, we had a date of marriage and a surname but little additional information. With Abigail, wife of Samuel, the circumstances are different. There is no marriage record, so we must approximate the date of marriage using our knowledge of Samuel and Abigail Gay's children's birthdates. Their eldest known child was a son Samuel, born at Roxbury, Massachusetts, on 24 February 1687/8. They had seven additional children, born at Roxbury and Swansea, Massachusetts. Unfortunately, we do not have recorded dates for all these children, but there was a daughter Hannah, born at Swansea on 30 April 1701, and apparently two children younger than that, and so perhaps born about 1703 and 1705. Based on the usual assumption that women were about 20 years old at first marriage, Abigail would have been born about 1667. She would then have been about 38 years old at the birth of her youngest child, well within the usual child-bearing range.

As a check upon this estimated date of birth for Abigail, we also have her age at death. After their period of residence at Swansea, the family had moved on to Lebanon, Connecticut, where Abigail died on 9 August 1744, "in her 78th year." Samuel outlived her and died there on 22 February 1753, "in his 92nd year." These dates are from the tombstone inscriptions in Exeter Cemetery, Lebanon. The formula "in her 78th year," if used correctly, would mean that Abigail was somewhere between her 77th and 78th birthday. This would place her birth between 9 August 1666 and 9 August 1667, which is an excellent match with the estimate derived from the birth date of her eldest child. (Note, by the way, that Samuel's death occurred in the year after the switch from the Julian to the Gregorian calendar, and so no resolution of a potential double-date is necessary.) See Figure 8.1 for the resulting linkage bundle.

We may gain some knowledge of the accuracy of the tombstone dates for Abigail by examining Samuel's dates more carefully, in other words, by employing source-analysis skills. The tombstone data would place Samuel's birth between 22 February 1661/2 and 22 February 1662/3. Samuel Gay was born at Dedham on 4 January 1662/3, so we have valuable evidence that whoever provided the information about Samuel Gay was an accurate reporter. Although we cannot be certain that the same person provided the information about both Samuel and Abigail, we have some evidence that members of this family had good knowledge of the family's vital events.

Having determined that Abigail was born in or very close to 1667, we next observe that she was probably a member of a Roxbury family. Samuel Gay was born in nearby Dedham, but his mother, Mary (Bridge) Gay, was from a Roxbury family, and Samuel's first two children were born at Roxbury. We hope, then, to find an Abigail born in Roxbury in or about 1667 who is not otherwise accounted for, and perhaps find evidence that this Abigail became the wife of Samuel Gay.

Fortunately for our purposes, both the town vital records and the church baptisms for Roxbury survive for the late 1660s and early 1670s, and they seem to be reasonably complete; that is, the record density for Roxbury

Linkage Bundle: Samuel Gay no. 1

On 24 February 1687/8, Samuel Gay, the eldest known child of Samuel and Abigail Gay, was born at Roxbury, Massachusetts.

On 9 August 1744, Abigail Gay, the wife of Samuel Gay, died at Lebanon, Connecticut, "in her 78th year."

Samuel and Abigail Gay of Roxbury, Swansea, and Lebanon had a son Joseph, a daughter Mehitable, and a grandson Philip.

Conclusion: By 1687 Samuel Gay, residing at Roxbury, had married a woman named Abigail, who was probably born about 1667.

Rationale: The first two records pertain to the same Abigail if the two records pertain to the same Samuel Gay; and if he had only one wife between 1687 and 1744.

The evidence for claiming the Samuel Gay in these two records was one man consists of a string of deeds, which first document the move of Samuel Gay and his family to Swansea about 1690, and then a second move, from Swansea to Lebanon, shortly after 1715.

On the second point, no evidence has been found indicating that Samuel had more than one wife. There is no earlier death record for an Abigail, wife of Samuel, during the period in question, nor is there a marriage for Samuel to a second Abigail in the same interval. Additionally, these two records are chronologically consistent with one another.

Having linked these two records, we estimate the birth year for Abigail. Since women generally made their first marriage in early New England at about the age of 20, Abigail would have been born about 1667, based solely on the first of these two records. A more accurate estimate of her birth year may be derived from the tombstone inscription, which states that she was between her 77th and 78th birthdays at her death, and therefore born in late 1666 or early 1667, a nice fit with the rougher estimate based on the birth of her first known child. (We will use the information on the names of children and grandchildren at a later point in the argument.)

Confidence: Almost certain.

Figure 8.1.

in this period is working in our favor. Examining all these records from 1662 to 1672, we find eleven Abigails born in Roxbury. Of these, four may be immediately eliminated as having died young or married someone other than Samuel Gay. Of the remaining seven, an additional four were born at the outer edges of the search range, and we will investigate them further only if the more likely candidates do not provide a solution. We are left with three possibilities, born in or close to 1667:

Abigail Wise, born 20 June 1666 and baptized 4 [*sic*] June 1666, daughter of Joseph Wise

Abigail Curtis, born 1 April 1667, daughter of Philip Curtis

Abigail Holbrook, born 13 May 1669, daughter of Daniel Holbrook

The charts in Figure 8.2 present this information in three additional partial networks, to show that in each case we have a small portion of the lives of three women named Abigail, and in each instance are looking to see if one of these partial networks might be woven into what we know of the family of Samuel Gay, to produce a more complete tapestry.

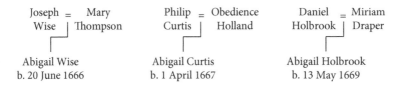

Figure 8.2.

Further examination of the Wise family demonstrated that Abigail Wise, daughter of Joseph, married about 1687 Adam Cogswell of Ipswich.[1] We are left, then, with two candidates to examine: Abigail Curtis and Abigail Holbrook.

In examining each of these candidates, we attend closely to several points of comparison, falling within three categories of circumstantial evidence: onomastics (study of proper names), chronology, and associations.

Onomastics (study of names): A number of given names appear among the descendants of Samuel Gay that are not otherwise seen at this early date in the Gay family, including Joseph, Mehitable, and Prudence among his children and Philip, Elisha, Simeon, and Gideon among his grandchildren. None of these names appears in the family of Abigail Holbrook. Three of the names, however, can be accounted for in the family of Abigail Curtis: her father was of course Philip, she had a brother Joseph, and her uncle Isaac had a daughter Mehitable, born before Samuel and Abigail Gay gave that name to one of their daughters.

Chronology: Comparing the known birth dates for the two candidates with the age at death for Abigail, wife of Samuel Gay, we observe that on 9 August 1744, Abigail Curtis would have been in her 78th year and Abigail Holbrook in her 76th year.

Associations: When we study the Curtis and Holbrook families, we discover three occasions on which members of the Gay and Curtis families interacted, but no such connections between the Gay and Holbrook families.

1. On 2 October 1682, Samuel Gay witnessed the will of Isaac Curtis, brother of Philip. This may have been Samuel, husband of Abigail, or his father Samuel. This record precedes by some years the marriage of the younger Samuel to Abigail, so probably arises through Mary (Bridge) Gay, mother of the younger Samuel. Thus, the Gay family and the Curtis family were certainly known to one another before the marriage of Samuel and Abigail.

2. On 1 August 1713, Mary Gay witnessed a deed in which the grantees were Benjamin and Obedience Gamlin. Obedience Gamlin was the remarried widow of Philip Curtis. Given the date, this Mary Gay could have been Mary (Bridge) Gay, or she could have been the daughter of Samuel and Abigail Gay, who was born about 1699, and was therefore just old enough to act legally as a witness.

3. On 22 July 1719, Mary Gay witnessed a deed in which the grantor was Obedience Gamlin, now a widow. By this date, Mary (Bridge) Gay was dead, so the witness in this instance was almost certainly the daughter of Samuel and Abigail Curtis, who was still single (and who in fact never married).

Looking back at our two candidates, Abigail Holbrook has nothing going for her. Not one of these three categories of evidence produces anything in her favor.

Abigail Curtis, however, comes out well ahead in all three categories: her family accounts for three of the "new" names among the children of Samuel and Abigail Gay; her year of birth matches exactly that calculated for the wife of Samuel Gay; and on at least three occasions the members of the Gay family witnessed legal documents executed by members of the Curtis family.

All this evidence, of course, is circumstantial, but altogether it is quite compelling. We are able, then, to state explicit reasons for concluding that the linkage bundles created around Abigail, wife of Samuel Gay, and around Abigail, daughter of Philip Curtis (Figure 8.3), pertain to the same individual. This conclusion has a confidence level of highly probable, inasmuch as all evidence points in the same direction, and the record density is favorable. The conclusion does not attain the level of "almost certain," since there remains the possibility that some other Abigail, perhaps omitted from the Roxbury records, perhaps from some other town, may actually have been Samuel's wife.

Linkage Bundle: Samuel Gay no. 2

Abigail Curtis, daughter of Philip and Obedience Curtis, was born at Roxbury, Massachusetts, on 1 April 1667.

The father of this Abigail Curtis was named Philip. She had a brother Joseph Curtis and a first cousin Mehitable Curtis.

On 2 October 1682, Samuel Gay witnessed the will of Isaac Curtis. (Isaac Curtis was uncle of Abigail Curtis.)

On 1 August 1713, Mary Gay witnessed a deed in which the grantees were Benjamin and Obedience Gamlin. (Obedience was mother of Abigail Curtis.)

On 22 July 1719, Mary Gay witnessed a deed in which the grantor was Obedience Gamlin, widow. (Obedience was mother of Abigail Curtis.)

Conclusion: An Abigail Curtis was born in Roxbury in 1667. Over a period of three decades, her family had several interactions with the Gay family.

Rationale: Our goal is to link the second, third, fourth and fifth of these records with the first, thus building up a picture of the life of this Abigail Curtis within the context of her birth family. Each item after the first is a complex conclusion representing the results of prior linkage analysis on the Curtis family. Although depicted here as a linkage bundle, this diagram actually represents a multi-level dossier for the Abigail Curtis born at Roxbury in 1667.

Confidence: Highly probable.

Figure 8.3.

In this one final linkage step, which creates the dossier for a single person (Figure 8.4), now designated as Abigail (Curtis) Gay, we have solved two reciprocal genealogical problems: we have provided parents for the wife of Samuel Gay and we have provided a spouse for the daughter of Philip Curtis.[2]

William White

The Second Fundamental Rule of genealogy may also be stood on its head. Not only do we demand that there be an explicit reason for stating that any two records pertain to a given individual, we also must work hard to be certain that we do not even inadvertently link two records that actually belong to two different individuals. This is, of course, the ever-present pitfall of "the name's the same."

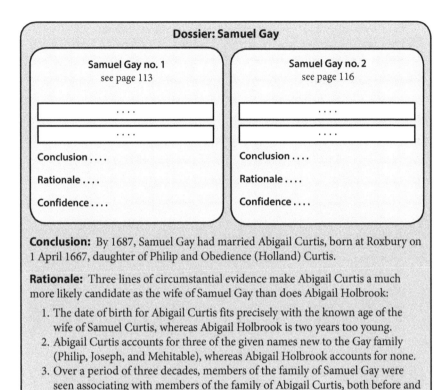

Dossier: Samuel Gay

Samuel Gay no. 1
see page 113

. . . .

. . . .

Conclusion . . . .

Rationale . . . .

Confidence . . . .

Samuel Gay no. 2
see page 116

. . . .

. . . .

Conclusion . . . .

Rationale . . . .

Confidence . . . .

Conclusion: By 1687, Samuel Gay had married Abigail Curtis, born at Roxbury on 1 April 1667, daughter of Philip and Obedience (Holland) Curtis.

Rationale: Three lines of circumstantial evidence make Abigail Curtis a much more likely candidate as the wife of Samuel Gay than does Abigail Holbrook:

1. The date of birth for Abigail Curtis fits precisely with the known age of the wife of Samuel Curtis, whereas Abigail Holbrook is two years too young.
2. Abigail Curtis accounts for three of the given names new to the Gay family (Philip, Joseph, and Mehitable), whereas Abigail Holbrook accounts for none.
3. Over a period of three decades, members of the family of Samuel Gay were seen associating with members of the family of Abigail Curtis, both before and after the marriage, whereas no such associations are seen for Abigail Holbrook.

Confidence: Probable.

Figure 8.4.

An example of this problem may be found in the early men of Essex County, Massachusetts, named William White. In his *Genealogical Dictionary of New England*, James Savage had three entries for men of that name in the towns of Ipswich and Newbury. By looking at the first of these entries, we can see where Savage went wrong.

> WILLIAM, Newbury, freeman 22 June 1642, had come from London in the Mary and John 1634, and first sat down at Ipswich, then removed probably in 1635 or 6, with many of his fellow-passengers, to Newbury, had John and James, the latter born says Coffin, about 1649; removed to Haverhill, there died 1690, aged 80.[3]

Savage explicitly identified only one of his sources, "Coffin," referring to the history of Newbury published in 1845 by Joshua Coffin. He relied on that non-contemporaneous source for only one of his statements in this entry, the age of supposed son James.

Let's first engage in some reverse linkage analysis, as discussed in Chapter Five, and list the separate statements in this entry for which we would wish to find the original source.

1. Passenger from London on *Mary and John*, 1634

2. First residence in New England at Ipswich

3. Removal to Newbury in 1635 or 1636

4. Freeman as a Newbury resident, 22 June 1642

5. Son John

6. Son James, born about 1649

7. Removal to Haverhill

8. Death at Haverhill in 1690, aged 80

Assuming that each of these statements is based on one or more recoverable records, the immediate objective is to determine whether Savage was correct in linking them together as all pertaining to the same individual. (As noted above, Savage included two other entries for men named William White who resided at Ipswich, each based on its own set of records.[4])

First Linkage Bundle

The passenger list for the *Mary & John*, compiled on 24 March 1633/4 and 26 March 1634, includes, under the earlier date, the name William White.[5] This record will be the nucleus of our first linkage bundle. Assuming that this vessel sailed for New England shortly after the date the list was compiled, William White and his fellow passengers would have arrived in the New World in late May or early June of 1634.

As Savage noted, a number of the passengers on the *Mary & John* settled first at Ipswich and then, when the neighboring town of Newbury was settled in 1635, were among the first settlers there. It is not surprising, therefore, to find records for a William White in Ipswich, the earliest being on 29 December 1634, when "a spring in question of difference between Mr. Nicholas Easton and William White was decided by . . . the committee appointed for that end."[6] William White was one of the commonest names to be found in England at the time of the Great Migration, and so not an unusual name in early New England. Since Nicholas Easton was also a passenger on the *Mary & John*, however, we may be reasonably confident that this record for a William White pertains to the 1634 passenger of that name. This first linkage decision creates at linkage bundle that ties together the first two statements in the list of those made by Savage in the William White entry presented opposite. (See Figure 8.5.)

> ### Linkage Bundle: William White no. 1
>
> ---
>
> On 24 March 1633/4, "William White" was enrolled at Southampton as a passenger for New England on the *Mary & John*.
>
> ---
>
> On 29 December 1634, a dispute "between Mr. Nicholas Easton and William White was decided by . . . the committee appointed for that end" at Ipswich.
>
> ---
>
> **Conclusion:** A man named William White sailed from England for New England in the spring of 1634 and, by the winter of the same year, was residing at Ipswich, Massachusetts.
>
> **Rationale:** The second of these records is the earliest appearance of the name William White at Ipswich. Nicholas Easton was also a passenger on the *Mary & John* (as were a number of other men who first appeared at Ipswich in 1634).
>
> **Confidence:** Highly probable.

Figure 8.5.

Other early records for William White at Ipswich describe the land grants made to him. On 26 January 1634/5, he received "twenty acres of land lying on the south side of this river."[7] On 20 April 1635, the town compiled a list of all the land granted to William White by that date: "An houselot . . . , also . . . a place to set a house . . . , also . . . twenty acres of land part meadow, part upland, lying on the east side of town, also . . . two hundred acres of land lying at the further Chebacco, bounded on the southeast by a creek that lies between it and Mr. Coggswell's land, bounded on the north by a great bare hill without trees."[8] The detailed descriptions of the last two parcels of land will turn out to be critical in sorting out the William Whites of early Essex County. To this point, there is no indication of a second William White in Ipswich, and so we add these two records to the linkage bundle that is beginning to take shape; see Figure 8.6. (Note that in this instance we are not creating a new linkage bundle but augmenting one already in existence.)

On 27 June 1638, "whereas William White of Ipswich, husbandman, had granted to him by the company of freemen twenty acres of land, lying at the east end of town, . . . being part meadow and part upland now the said William White hath sold unto Thomas Treadwell of Ipswich all the said twenty acres of meadow and upland lying and bounded as above written, for which land the said Thomas Treadwell hath given and paid in exchange, six acres of planting ground lying on the east side of the great hill commonly called Heartbreak Hill."[9] Based on the description of the land, we may be confident that the William White of this record is the same as the man of that name of the 20 April 1635, and so, if the record of 20 April 1635 pertains to the 1634 passenger, then so must this deed of 27 June 1638.

Linkage Bundle: William White no. 1A

On 24 March 1633/4, "William White" was enrolled at Southampton as a passenger for New England on the *Mary & John*.

On 29 December 1634, a dispute "between Mr. Nicholas Easton and William White was decided by . . . the committee appointed for that end" at Ipswich.

On 26 January 1634/5, the town of Ipswich "granted unto William White twenty acres of land lying on the south side of this river."

On 20 April 1635, the town of Ipswich "granted to William White an house lot . . . , also . . . a place to set a house . . . , also . . . twenty acres of land part meadow, part upland, lying on the east side of town, also . . . two hundred acres of land lying at the further Chebacco, bounded on the southeast by a creek that lies between it and Mr. Coggswell's land, bounded on the north by a great bare hill without trees."

Conclusion: A man named William White sailed from England for New England in the spring of 1634 and, by the winter of the same year, was residing at Ipswich, Massachusetts. Early in 1635 he began to receive grants of land from the town.

Rationale: Building on conclusions in the earlier version of this linkage bundle, we observe that land grants of this sort would be appropriate for a man who had just arrived in Ipswich. There is no indication that there were two men by the name of William White in Ipswich at this time.

Confidence: Highly probable.

Figure 8.6.

This exchange of land between William White and Thomas Treadwell states explicitly that William White was resident of Ipswich at the time of the 1635 deed, but not that he was living there in 1638. However, since the land that White received in exchange was also in Ipswich, his continued residence in that town seems highly likely. Here the story we are building departs from that prepared by Savage, who thought that the 1634 passenger had, after a brief residence at Ipswich, moved on to Newbury by 1635 or 1636.

Second Linkage Bundle

At this point, we set aside the linkage bundle we have been building for the 1634 passenger and look for evidence of a William White at Newbury. No man of this name appears in the early town meeting records of Newbury, which are reasonably complete for the late 1630s. William White does appear in a list of Newbury proprietors dated 7 December 1642,[10] but nowhere else in the early lists of Newbury landholding.

We can with reasonable confidence place a William White in Newbury on 22 June 1642, when six men were admitted to Massachusetts Bay freemanship. Four of these men (Henry Palmer, Joseph Peasley, William Titcomb, and Thomas Dow) were certainly Newbury residents on that date and a fifth (Richard Pid) may also have been of that town (if we assume that this name, not otherwise seen in New England, was a garbled version of Richard Fitz). The remaining name in this list of freemen, fifth in the sequence of six, was William White, and so we conclude that he also was of Newbury on that date.

On 10 April 1650, "William Easto of Hampton . . . , husbandman," sold to "William White of Haverhill, planter, . . . my house and lot with all the appurtenances thereunto belonging, as upland, marsh or meadow, that is mine, excepting four acres sold unto Mr. John Oliver . . . in the town of Newbury."[11] On 6 July 1650, "whereas William White, lately of Newbery . . . , yeoman, . . . did heretofore sell unto Thomas Jones, then of Newbery, now of Charlestowne, butcher, all his houselot of four acres . . . in Newbery aforesaid, as it is next to the land of Robert Coker, with twelve acres of salt marsh below Great Pine Island, witness now these presents, that the said Thomas Jones long since in the year 1641 or 1642 . . . did sell all that abovementioned house, houselot, with twelve acres of salt marsh below Great Pine Island with all the privileges thereto belonging, to William Elnsly of Newbery aforesaid."[12] On 8 April 1679, "John Emerie Sr., aged about eighty-one years, testified that about forty years ago he saw laid out to William Estow then living in Nuberie a four-acre lot being a houselot and twelve acres of meadow, bounded by Great Pine Island creek southerly, . . . which land said Estow sold to William White, and White to Tho[mas] Jones of Hampton, and Jones to deponent for William Ilsly Sr., who has peacably enjoyed it from 1643 to date."[13]

If we interpret the 1650 deed from Eastow to White to be a belated confirmation of a sale made about ten years earlier, as testified to by John Emery in 1679, then all three documents fall into line. They place a William White in Newbury about 1641 or 1642 (which is consistent with the record of William White as a freeman and proprietor at Newbury in 1642), and they further indicate that by 1650 (and probably earlier) this William White was a resident of Haverhill. So, we have created a second linkage bundle (Figure 8.7), consisting of a record of freemanship, a record of proprietorship, two deeds, and a deposition, that tell the story of a William White who was in Newbury by 1642 and then moved on to Haverhill by the end of the 1640s. This includes the third, fourth, and seventh of the statements that we extracted from Savage's first William White entry.

Linkage Bundle: William White no. 2

On 22 June 1642, William White of Newbury was admitted as a freeman of Massachusetts Bay. (Of the six men admitted as freemen that day, the five other than William White are known to have been Newbury residents at the time, implying that William White was also of Newbury.)

On 7 December 1642, William White was included in a list of proprietors of Newbury land.

On 10 April 1650, "William Easto of Hampton . . . husbandman" sold to "William White of Haverhill, planter," land in Newbury.

On 6 July 1650, "whereas William White, lately of Newbery . . . , yeoman, . . . did heretofore sell unto Thomas Jones, then of Newbery, now of Charlestowne, butcher," and "the said Thomas Jones long since in the year 1641 or 1642" sold the same land to "William Elnsly of Newbery aforesaid."

On 8 April 1679, John Emery Senior deposed that "about forty years ago . . . William Estow then living in Nuberie . . . sold [land] to William White, and White to Thomas Jones of Hampton, and Jones to William Ilsly Sr., who has peacably enjoyed it from 1643 to date."

Conclusion: The first appearance of a man named William White in Newbury, Massachusetts, was in 1642. He soon removed to Haverhill, Massachusetts.

Rationale: The first record marks the first appearance of a William White in Newbury records.

The second record, from just a few months later, almost certainly pertains to the same man, employing our usual argument that there are no indications of two men of the name in town in that year.

The fourth and fifth records, although dated in 1650 and 1679, refer to events in Newbury in the early 1640s, very close to the time of the first two records. These two records clearly refer to the same piece of land and to the same land transaction.

For the third record to connect to the fourth and fifth, we make the claim that this also referred to the same piece of land and the same land transaction, and is a confirmation by William Eastow of the sale of nearly a decade earlier.

If we accept that interpretation, then all five records describe events involving a William White in Newbury in 1642 and 1643. Once we accept that all five records pertain to one man named William White, then the conclusion that he soon moved from Newbury to Haverhill is straightforward.

Confidence: Highly probable.

Figure 8.7.

Savage created his first William White entry by combining the two linkage bundles that we have created here. Was he justified in linking those two bundles of records to form a dossier for a William White of Ipswich, Newbury, and Haverhill? The following two lines of reasoning lead to the conclusion that he was not.

First, without rehearsing all the details behind the reasoning, an additional linkage bundle may be developed, for the name William White in Haverhill, which shows a man of that name there continuously from 1650 until his death at Haverhill on 28 September 1690, "aged about 80 years." This William White had a son John. We may confidently link this additional linkage bundle, which includes Savage's fifth and eighth statements, to the second linkage bundle, thus tracing the life of this man from 1642 to 1690. (We do not provide a diagram for this additional linkage bundle.)

Third Linkage Bundle

Second, when we return to Ipswich records, we find a number of additional items for the name William White, which show a man of that name in town until his death on 25 August 1684. Most important, on 2 October 1647, "William White of Ipswich" mortgaged to "Ralfe Dix of the same town, fisherman, . . . my farm lying and being in Ipswich aforesaid at Chebaco, containing by estimation 200 acres."[14] This farm would appear to be the same farm granted to William White by early 1635, which we have already associated with the 1634 passenger.

This assumption is greatly strengthened by a deed of 6 April 1691, in which "James White of Ipswich" confirmed unto William Goodhue Junior a parcel of land, "in consideration that my father William White" had sold this parcel unto three other Ipswich men, who then sold the land to Goodhue; this piece of land is described in part as "fourscore & two acres . . . bounded in form following, viz: on the southeast by a creek, next Cogswell's farm, on the southwest by the common of Ipswich & land of the ministry of Chebacco."[15] Despite the passage of more than half a century, this large tract of land is recognizable as a large part of the farm granted to William White in 1635; the elements in common are the size of the parcel, the location in Chebacco (the eastern part of Ipswich, adjacent to Gloucester), and the adjacency to Mr. Cogswell's farm.

We have, therefore, created a third linkage bundle (Figure 8.8), for a William White in Ipswich from the 1640s until his death in 1684. Based on the history of the farm granted to William White in 1635, we may now link this third bundle to the augmented first bundle created above, thus describing the life of a single William White in Ipswich from 1634 to 1684. This third bundle includes the sixth statement from Savage's entry, so we have now accounted for all portions of this first William White in Savage's accounting.

On 2 October 1647, "William White of Ipswich" mortgaged to "Ralfe Dix of the same town, fisherman, . . . my farm . . . in Ipswich aforesaid at Chebaco, containing by estimation 200 acres."

William White died at Ipswich on 25 August 1684.

On 6 April 1691, "James White of Ipswich" confirmed to William Goodhue that "my father William White" in 1658 sold to three men land that those same three men then sold to Goodhue; the land in question contained "fourscore and two acres . . . bounded . . . on the southeast by a creek, next Mr. Cogswell's farm, on the southwest by the common of Ipswich & land of the ministry in Chebacco."

Conclusion: A man named William White resided in Ipswich from 1647 until his death in 1684 and had a son named James.

Rationale: The linkage of the first and third of these records requires a detailed analysis of the land being conveyed in each. The land in both instances is in the Chebacco section of Ipswich and abuts the farm of John Cogswell. In the 1691 deed, James White is confirming an action taken by his father, implying that his father had died between 1658 and 1691. The 1684 death date for a William White is the only one in Ipswich during that period, and there are no records which suggest the presence of more than one William White during the period in question.

Confidence: Highly probable.

Figure 8.8.

By tying the first linkage bundle to the third, we exclude the possibility that this man can be the same as the William White of Newbury and Haverhill described above. (This entire problem is elaborated in much

Chronological lists as analytic tools

A technique that can be especially helpful in sorting out two or more people of the same name is to compile a simple chronological list of *all* the occurrences of that name. Such a list may possibly highlight instances in which two or more records for that name are in direct conflict and cannot possibly be for the same person. When you find such a conflicting pair of records, each can be employed as the seed crystal for distinct linkage bundles that may lead to the solution of the problem. In 1981 Ruth Wilder Sherman employed this technique in reverse manner as part of her argument that a man named William Drinkwater from 1700 to 1722 was identical with a man named Warren Drinkwater from 1723 until his death sometime after 1734.[16]

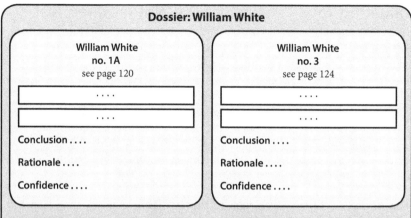

Dossier: William White

> **William White**
> **no. 1A**
> see page 120
>
> ....
>
> ....
>
> Conclusion ....
>
> Rationale ....
>
> Confidence ....

> **William White**
> **no. 3**
> see page 124
>
> ....
>
> ....
>
> Conclusion ....
>
> Rationale ....
>
> Confidence ....

Conclusion: William White sailed for New England in 1634, settled immediately at Ipswich, and resided there until his death in 1684. He is distinct from the William White who appeared at Newbury in 1642 and soon moved to Haverhill. William White of Ipswich had a son James White.

Rationale: The principal evidence tying these two linkage bundles together is the identification of the 200-acre parcel of land granted to William White in 1635 with 200-acre farm mortgaged by William White in 1647, followed by the sale of portions of that farm by William White in 1658 and the confirmation of that sale in 1691 by his son James White. This conclusion is supported by other records for the name William White in Ipswich, which are chronologically and otherwise consistent with there being but one William White in Ipswich from 1634 to 1684, and with the dossier created for another William White who was briefly at Newbury in 1642 and 1643 and then resided at Haverhill until his death in 1690.

Confidence: Highly probable.

Figure 8.9.

greater detail in the Great Migration sketch of William White.[17]) Thus, by applying the same rules and the same procedure that we have employed in identifying spouses and parents, we have carefully separated myriad records that pertain to two different individuals, thus avoiding falling into the "name's the same" fallacy. Figure 8.9 presents the dossier that describes William White of Ipswich.

Evaluating Your Conclusion: The White Queen Test

Once you have reached a genealogical conclusion, with whatever degree of confidence, you should apply one final test, the White Queen Test, named for the White Queen in Lewis Carroll's *Alice Through the Looking Glass*. The White Queen assured Alice that she was quite capable of believing six impossible things before breakfast. In this test, you emulate the White Queen by turning your conclusion on its head and asking what you would have to believe if the conclusion were *untrue*. As the propositions you must believe in order to *disprove* your hypothesis become more and more unbelievable (to anyone but the White Queen), so your proposed conclusion gains in strength.

As an example, let's take the English origin of John Hunting, who settled in Dedham, Massachusetts, in 1638.[18] As is our usual procedure, we first gather what we know about this man once he has arrived in New England. He had a wife, Esther, and at least five children born in England: son John and daughters Mary, Margaret, Esther, and Elizabeth. Based on evidence from New England, mostly their dates of marriage, these children were born in the late 1620s and early 1630s— suggesting that John Hunting himself was born not far from 1600.

In many instances of early migration to New England, information of this sort is all we have to work with. For John Hunting and his family, however, we have much more. In her will of 4 January 1675/6, Hester Hunting, wife of John Hunting, included a bequest to "my loving brother Francis Seaborne in old England." Further research unearthed the marriage of John Hunting and Hester Seaborne at Wramplingham, Norfolk, on 28 June 1624. (The names Esther and Hester were interchangeable in the seventeenth century.)

Wramplingham is in south-central Norfolk, a likely origin for an early Dedham, Massachusetts, family, as many of the immigrants to that town in the late 1630s were from southern Norfolk and northern Suffolk. A survey of records in that part of England reveals that the Hunting surname was common in a number of parishes in north-central Suffolk, including at Hoxne, Thrandeston, and Oakley. The baptism of a John Hunting, son of William and Margaret, at Thrandeston on 24 January 1601/2 is a good match for the immigrant to New England. Baptisms for Mary and Margaret, daughters of John Hunting, were discovered at nearby Hoxne in 1626 and 1628, and of Esther, Elizabeth, and John, children of John Hunting, at Oakley in 1631, 1634, and 1636. Finally, "Margaret Hunting of Hoxne . . . , widow," mother of the John Hunting baptized at Thrandeston, in her will of 25 October 1648, included a bequest to "John Hunting of New England my son."

The identification of the English origin of John Hunting and his family presented here in outline is about as strong and solid as it gets. Given the close match of the names and baptismal dates of the children in Norfolk with what is known of the family in New England, the identification would be solid even without the will of Margaret Hunting.

In this case, then, in order to apply the White Queen Test, you would say, "What do I have to believe to state that John Hunting in New England with wife Esther and these five children is *not* the same one whose records are found in Oakley and in Hoxne and whose mother says he is in New England?" And you have to believe a lot of very strange things.

You have to believe, first of all, that there were two people who met these criteria— not just two John Huntings, but two with wife Esther and all of these children. You have to believe that there were two of them who came to New England and one of them left no records; that the one from Hoxne and Oakley came to New England as his mother's will says that he did, but that he just evaporated; and that the other one appeared out of nowhere with no other record that we can find. Or you have to believe that there were two John Huntings in Hoxne and Oakley, one of whom shows up in the records and the other of whom doesn't, and it is the one who doesn't who comes to New England. Or some other equally unlikely story.

In other words, you try to destroy your own conclusion, and when you begin to have to generate these fairytales to say that your conclusion is not correct, then the more confident you may be that your conclusion *is* correct. The probability of the correctness of your conclusion is proportional to the improbability, even the impossibility, of the stories generated by the White Queen Test.

Summary

In this chapter we have examined a number of concepts which bear on the problem-solving step of problem resolution. In one way or another, most of these concepts derive from the Second Fundamental Rule.

- Our primary goal in genealogical research is adding to our knowledge of the genealogical definition of an individual, that is, of providing some evidence that will lead to the identification of that person's parents, spouses and children.

- The solution of a genealogical problem is the result of joining two or more linkage bundles or dossiers.

- The solution of any given genealogical problem is the reciprocal of some other problem; for example, identifying someone's parents simultaneously adds to the genealogical definition of one of the children of those parents.

Appendixes

Appendix A

Glossary

data collection: The gathering of information from **records** already examined by others or from **sources** not previously exploited. This is the third step in the problem-solving sequence. [Chapter Six]

dossier: A collection of two or more **linkage bundles** which, through the application of **linkage analysis**, you have determined to pertain to the same individual. [Chapter Three]

First Fundamental Rule: All statements must be based only on accurately reported, carefully documented, and exhaustively analyzed records. [Overview]

genealogically defined: Any person is **genealogically defined** if we have at least one piece of evidence that will lead to the identification of his or her parents, one piece of evidence for each spouse, and one piece of evidence for each child. [Chapter Four]

generic external knowledge: Data and thought processes that are applicable across the board, regardless of the time and place you are researching. [Chapter Two]

linkage analysis: The comparison of two or more **records**, or two or more **linkage bundles**, with a goal of determining whether or not they pertain to the same individual. As part of this process, you provide a **rationale** for your decisions. [Chapter Three]

linkage bundle: A collection of two or more **records** which, through the application of **linkage analysis**, you have determined to pertain to the same individual. [Chapter Three]

list analysis: A variety of **source analysis** that aims to determine the date of a list, or the dates of the entries within a list, when the date of that list is unknown or uncertain. [Chapter One]

points of comparison: The minimal elements that are considered when creating linkage bundles, comprising a wide range of markers, including name, age, residence, occupation, and many others. Generally, no single marker will be sufficient for linking two items. [Chapter Three]

problem analysis: The second step in the problem-solving sequence. A study of a genealogical problem, consisting of three steps: performing a literature search, analyzing previous conclusions, and generating a **data collection plan**. [Chapter Five]

problem resolution: The final step in the problem-solving sequence, arising from a series of linkage decisions. [Chapter Eight]

problem selection: Accurate definition of the problem to be studied and the questions that are to be answered; the first step in the overall problem-solving sequence. [Chapter Four]

rationale: Narrative that presents the researcher's arguments for creating a **linkage bundle**. [Chapter Three]

record: That portion of a **source** which pertains to a single event. [Chapter Two]

record analysis: The analysis of a set of records, with the goal of determining—by posing a number of questions—the **substance** in that record, and the **reliability** of that substance, in preparation for **linkage analysis**. [Chapter Two]

record density: The relative number of records available from time to time and place to place, at all jurisdictional levels, determined by three variables: the variety of types of sources created; the number of those sources that have survived; and the completeness of coverage of each of those sources. Record density will determine the value to place on individual records in the construction of linkage bundles. [Chapter Six]

reliability: The relative value, for the purpose of making linkage decisions, of the substance, that is, of the statements of fact, extracted from the records being analyzed. [Chapter One]

resolution: *See* **Problem resolution.**

reverse linkage analysis: A version of linkage analysis in which you begin with the conclusions and attempt to untangle and delineate the linkage decisions that were made to arrive at these conclusions. [Chapter Five]

Second Fundamental Rule: You must have a sound, explicit reason for saying that any two individual records refer to the same person. [Overview]

source: A coherent collection of **records** created by a single jurisdiction or a single author for a defined purpose. [Chapter One]

source analysis: The act of posing a number of questions to a **source**, with the goal of determining the **substance** contained in that source, and the **reliability** of that substance, in preparation for **record analysis**. [Chapter One]

specific external knowledge: Information external to the specific records being analyzed that supports the linkage decisions and that varies from time to time and place to place. [Chapter Two]

substance: The various statements of fact presented by a given **record**: the names, dates, places, and relationships that will be of value when linking two or more records together. [Chapter One]

synthesis: The examination of two or more **linkage bundles** or **dossiers** that you suspect belong to the same person. This is the fourth step in the problem-solving sequence. [Chapter Seven]

Appendix B

The Three Paradigms

Different scholarly disciplines rely on different protocols for evaluating evidence and for arriving at conclusions based on that evidence. This appendix discusses three such paradigms that have at various times been promoted as being useful and relevant to genealogists. Diplomatics, a variant of the third paradigm, is the most appropriate for genealogical research.

The Legal Model

The method of analyzing evidence most frequently promoted for genealogists in the not-so-distant past was modeled upon the law. This should not be surprising, as so many of the documents that genealogists collect are of a legal nature, filed in a courthouse somewhere. And genealogists, like lawyers and other court officials, spend their time collecting and evaluating evidence, and then using that evidence to prove a case.

Legal reasoning and legal categories have been recommended both for evaluating evidence (e.g., the hearsay rule), and for proving a case (preponderance of the evidence). But the legal model has many shortcomings when we are studying the distant past.

The most comprehensive presentation of this model of genealogical research was published by Noel C. Stevenson, a lawyer and genealogist, in *Genealogical Evidence: A Guide to the Standard of Proof Relating to Pedigrees, Ancestry, Heirship and Family History* (Laguna Hills, Calif.: Aegean Park Press, 1979). Stevenson set forth his views in Part IV, "Simplified Rules of Evidence," comprising two chapters: Chapter 21, "Rules of Evidence Applied to Genealogy" (pp. 179–188); and Chapter 22, "Hearsay Evidence" (pp. 189–200). He discusses at length such legal principles as best evidence, hearsay evidence (and exceptions thereto), and the ancient document rule.

Genealogists have in the past been directed to use the legal standard of proof that applies to civil cases, in which the determination is made on the basis of the preponderance of the evidence. That would require modeling genealogical research along the lines of a civil lawsuit, in which one party confronts another, and there must be a winner and a loser. With the exception of such cases as a dispute over inheritance, this is not the situation that confronts most genealogists. Rather, in solving a problem of ancestry, there may be one, two, or a dozen candidates for a position on the pedigree chart—or none. Furthermore, determination by the preponderance of evidence requires only the narrowest of margins to be successful, just barely more than fifty percent. Genealogists frequently attain a much higher level of certainty, and should never be satisfied with a simple preponderance in the legal sense.

The divergences between legal and genealogical research go beyond this. In the law, best evidence is always the direct testimony of an eyewitness to the facts in question. With some exceptions, relating mostly to oral testimony of living persons about the most recent generations, genealogists can never obtain "best evidence" in the strict legal sense. The vast majority of the genealogist's work relies on written documents, prepared by persons long deceased. These come under the hearsay rule in law, and so the genealogist, in attempting to emulate the law, must search for an exception to the hearsay rule in order to admit a piece of evidence. An intellectual pursuit that relies almost wholly on exceptions to rules of evidence has a very precarious existence, and this is what genealogy becomes if it tries to follow too closely the rules of law. Because genealogy depends almost totally on written records, a set of rules of evidence developed for just that sort of record would seem more appropriate, which is why a historical rather than a legal model should be sought for genealogical research.

This is not to say that the genealogist can afford to be ignorant of the law. We must be able to interpret the records that we encounter, and when these are legal records, we must have at hand a good legal dictionary, and, if one exists, a history of the law for the time and place we are studying. In this volume such information has been designated as a variety of **specific external knowledge** (see Chapter Two).

The Scientific Model

A second approach to evaluating evidence, not advocated as often in genealogical circles as the legal paradigm, is the scientific method. Although some features of this system are useful to the genealogist, the scientific method is for the most part even less amenable to historical subjects than the law.

So long as we construe such an appeal broadly, in the sense that we should reach our conclusions on the basis of consistent and objective principles, no one would object. But if the call for scientific genealogy means the transferral to genealogy of the detailed procedures of the natural sciences, such as physics and chemistry, then we are on dangerous ground.

A central feature of scientific methodology is the replicable experiment, in which different scientists, if they follow the same set of instructions, can carry out the same experiment and arrive at the same conclusions. But human beings are not indistinguishable atoms that can be subjected to repeated experiments, and this approach is not available to the genealogist.

Not all of science proceeds in this manner, such as evolutionary biology, for example. In this case the objects of investigation can be unique individuals, with a history that does not allow for replicable experiments. But it is just this feature, the unique history of an individual, that makes these fields of study as much historical as scientific; and we should be reminded thereby that genealogy is a historical, and not a scientific, discipline.

There is, however, one aspect of scientific methodology that may be applied successfully, and this is the development and testing of hypotheses. (For a good general treatment of hypothesis, and of the scientific method overall, see W. I. B. Beveridge, *The Art of Scientific Investigation* [Caldwell, N.J.: Blackburn Press, 2004]). In genealogy, this may take the form of proposing one particular set of parents for the person whose ancestry we are tracing, and then collecting evidence on that set of parents with a view toward proving or disproving the hypothesis. We have used this approach earlier in this volume in the case study of the identification of the wife of Samuel Gay (see Chapter Eight). The hypothesis must be treated carefully, and not allowed to become a fixed idea that interferes with the job at hand. As Beveridge counsels, "Hypotheses should be used as tools to uncover new facts rather than as ends in themselves" (p. 63).

The Historico-Literary Model

A third way of evaluating evidence—which genealogists do not discuss as much as the previous models but which they constantly use in an implicit fashion—is the literary-historical approach. This method of analyzing evidence takes many forms, depending on the particular historical subject under study. Each of these variants has in common the assumptions that our knowledge is based on written documents, and that our study of them must take into account the development of the actors in historical context.

Perhaps the earliest form of the historico-literary method was that known as diplomatics. The word *diplomatics* is derived from *diploma,* in medieval times the Latin word for an official charter or other document issued by a king or head of government, under his seal. Diplomatics proceeds by submitting each document of interest to a series of questions, and using the answers to those questions to evaluate the evidence. A brief introduction to this subject may be found in

"Diplomatic Studies," by Leonard E. Boyle, in *Medieval Studies: An Introduction*, James M. Powell, ed. (Syracuse, N.Y.: Syracuse University Press, 1976), 69–101. A more detailed exposition of this approach may be found in *Diplomatics: New Uses for an Old Science* by Luciana Duranti (Lanham, Md.: Scarecrow Press, 1998).

Almost as old as diplomatics is the critical study of the Bible, which has taken on its own distinctive methods and terminology. Two useful introductions to this variant of the historico-literary method are Edgar Krentz, *The Historical-Critical Method* (Eugene, Ore.: Wipf and Stock, 2002), and Richard N. Soulen, *Handbook of Biblical Criticism* (Atlanta: John Knox Press, 1976).

A more general outline of the historico-literary mode of criticism, with strong emphasis on modern literature, may be found in Richard D. Altick, *The Art of Literary Research* (New York: W.W. Norton & Co., 1963). Altick has written widely on this and closely related subjects, and any of his books is both entertaining and instructive.

Within the historico-literary paradigm, diplomatics, because of its emphasis on government documents, comes closest to the interests of genealogists. In the present volume, therefore, I have chosen to employ an extended version of diplomatics in our analysis of sources and records. Rather than attempt to classify each document rigidly as primary or secondary, or to describe each piece of evidence as direct or circumstantial, the diplomatist poses a series of questions to each source and each record, slowly learning in that process the value of the evidence it contains.

Appendix C

GENTECH Genealogical Data Model

From 1996 until 2000 I had the pleasure and the privilege of being a member of the Lexicon Working Group, which created the GENTECH Genealogical Data Model (GDM). The goal of the Lexicon Project, created jointly by GENTECH and the Federation of Genealogical Societies, was "to define genealogical data for the purpose of facilitating data exchange among genealogists." After some time spent in directly developing a lexicon of genealogical terms, the group "decided that the effort would be better served by defining genealogical data in the context of a logical data model."[1]

The GDM is described in a hundred-page text document and displayed in a form known as an entity-relation diagram. The entire model is arranged as three interconnected components, devoted to administration, evidence, and conclusions. The latter section is most closely pertinent to the subject matter of the present volume, and a portion of that diagram is displayed on the next page.

For a full explanation of this portion of the model, refer to the report referenced above. For the purposes of this volume, note that the ASSERTION entity is roughly equivalent to our linkage bundles. In building an ASSERTION, we take two or more records ("from SOURCE") or two or more other linkage bundles ("from ASSERTION") and join them into a higher-level ASSERTION. The two records or two linkage bundles are referenced as "Subject1-Type" and "Subject2-Type." In joining these two items, we are required to provide a "rationale," which the GDM defines as "narrative that explains the researcher's basis for the assertion." We have borrowed this concept and altered the definition in a few places, but the underlying idea remains the same.

The ASSERTION-ASSERTION entity permits recursion, so that lower-level ASSERTIONS (linkage bundles) may be built up into higher-level ASSERTIONS (dossiers), without limit. This corresponds to the synthesis step in the problem-solving sequence, as described in Chapter Seven.

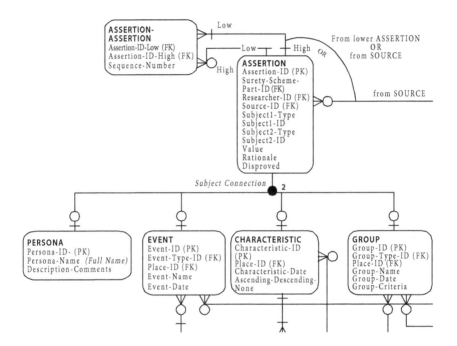

(The equation of our records or linkage bundles with "Subject1-Type" and Subject2-Type" of the GDM is not exact, as the latter refer to selected components of the records, more or less equivalent to our points of comparison. The resulting structures, however, are equivalent, and have the same import.)

Appendix D

Forgery

Although genealogists do not often come across forged documents in their research, such documents do occasionally intrude. Some of the signs of forgeries are internal contradictions, problems with the ink and the handwriting, and anachronisms, in which, for example, place names are used many years before they were actually employed for a given location. Motivation for forging one or two documents in a lawsuit—for example, to gain benefit for one side—can be alluring, and so the possibility of forgery should always be considered, but judiciously. Two examples are provided here.

➤ Example One: Fabricated Records

Research on the English settlement of southwestern Pennsylvania and neighboring areas in the late eighteenth century is notoriously difficult. In 1945 W. F. Horn, under the auspices of the Greene County [Pennsylvania] Historical Society, published *The Horn Papers: Early Westward Movement on the Monongahela and Upper Ohio, 1765–1795*, a three-volume set. The first volume contained transcripts of newly discovered, or at least newly revealed, early court dockets, private diaries, maps, and other documents, along with Horn's modern commentaries on these sources. The second volume consisted of hundreds of genealogies of early settlers of the area, compiled by Horn, based on the material in the first volume. And the third volume held copies of warrant, survey, and patent maps for three counties in southwestern Pennsylvania, prepared "for abstractors of titles and business firms, such as coal companies seeking a complete chain of title," supplied by the state of Pennsylvania.

In July 1946 Julian P. Boyd published a letter questioning the authenticity of some of the material in the first two volumes. Almost immediately a committee was established, sponsored by The Institute of Early American History and Culture, and given the task of exploring the charges made by Boyd.

In the October 1947 issue of the *William and Mary Quarterly*, the committee issued its report, which declared that "the documents printed in *The Horn Papers* show numerous signs of being fabrications." They based this conclusion on the presence of anachronistic words and phrases, of historically incorrect statements, and of internal contradictions. In addition, physical examination of the supposed "original" sources showed that the ink and paper would not have been used in the late eighteenth century, but were of late nineteenth- and even twentieth-century origin. The committee declared that the material in the third volume did not suffer from these defects, but was reliable and valuable.

The investigators did not find that the perpetrators of this forgery, whoever they may have been, produced this invented source material for any pecuniary advantage, or in support of any legal proceedings. They suggest that the materials may have been created by W. F. Horn's grandfather sometime in the mid-nineteenth century for the amusement of his family.[1]

Example Two: Combination of Forged and Genuine

In the New Hampshire State Archives rests a volume with the title "Book I, Province Records, 1631–1650," which contains a number of loose documents that in the nineteenth century were mounted and bound. New Hampshire did not, of course, exist as a separate province or colony during the years covered by this collection of papers. The towns that ended up in New Hampshire (Portsmouth, Dover, Exeter, and Hampton) were either independent governments or subordinate to Massachusetts Bay during these years.

The first twenty-nine of these documents have been published in the first volume of *New Hampshire Provincial Papers* and are referred to as the "Gibbins Papers," for Ambrose Gibbins, who managed the affairs of Captain John Mason on the Piscataqua.[2] In presenting material from this source, Noyes, Libby, and Davis in *Genealogical Dictionary of Maine and New Hampshire* state that the names and other information are "collated from papers saved by Mr. Ambrose Gibbins [and other sources]. . . . (Six forged documents now kept with the Gibbins papers are disregarded.)"[3] Unfortunately, these three authors do not identify these six documents.

Four of the forged documents are, however, easily identified, mostly from internal evidence. The first in the series that is clearly faulty is No. 17, which purports to be an agreement, dated 13 August 1633, between Captain Walter Neale and Captain Thomas Wiggin as to the division of lands in the various patents along the Piscataqua.[4] James Savage was among the earliest to point out the problems with this agreement. The letter refers to the towns of Northam (a transient name for Dover) and

Portsmouth. But Dover did not acquire the name of Northam until 1640, and the town now known as Portsmouth was Strawbery Banke until about 1651. Also, Savage noted that, very inconveniently, on the date of the agreement Neale was in England, about to return to the Piscataqua, and Wiggin had taken ship for England just a few days earlier.[5]

Having impeached this item, the two papers included in item No. 24, and also the letter dated 10 April 1636, printed as item No. 25, must also be forgeries.[6] These documents were created and smuggled into the Gibbins Papers late in the seventeenth century, in an attempt to support the claims of the heirs of Capt. John Mason to much of the land between the Piscataqua and the Merrimack. The remaining items in the Gibbins Papers appear to be genuine, contemporary records, mostly recording the business activities of Gibbins and those who worked under him at the various settlements along the Piscataqua.

Notes

Chapter One

1. *Nature,* 307 (1984):318.
2. *A Tribute to John Insley Coddington on the Occasion of the Fortieth Anniversary of the American Society of Genealogists,* Neil D. Thompson and Robert Charles Anderson, eds. (New York, 1980), 31–46.
3. *The Source: A Guidebook of American Genealogy,* Loretto Dennis Szucs and Sandra Hargreaves Luebking, eds., 3rd ed. (Provo, Utah, 2006), 161–163.
4. *The American Genealogist,* 62:242–244.
5. *The New York Genealogical and Biographical Record,* 138:5–13.
6. Elizabeth Pearson White, *John Howland of the Mayflower,* Volume 1 (Camden, Maine, 1990), 514–515. In the same year this book was published, White and two other authors prepared a separate treatment of this family and settled on the name Faith: *The American Genealogist* 65:214-18.
7. Windham Probate District File #2578.
8. Windham Probate District Record Book 5:489–491.
9. New London Probate District File #3360.
10. New London Probate District Book G: 362.
11. H. Don Cameron, "The Upside-down Cladogram: Problems in Manuscript Affiliation," in Henry M. Hoenigswald and Linda F. Wiener, *Biological Metaphor and Cladistic Classification: An Interdisciplinary Perspective* (Philadelphia, 1987), 227–242.
12. Richard S. Dunn, James Savage, and Laetitia Yeandle, eds., *The Journal of John Winthrop, 1630–1649* (Cambridge and London, 1996). [hereafter *Winthrop Journal*]
13. *Winthrop Journal,* pp. xx–xxvii.
14. *The New York Genealogical and Biographical Record,* 140:261–271.
15. *New England Historical and Genealogical Register,* 121:81 [hereafter *Register*].
16. *Great Migration Newsletter,* 6:4–5.
17. *The Record of Baptisms, Marriages and Deaths . . . from the Church Records in the Town of Dedham, Massachusetts, 1638–1845 . . . ,* Don Gleason Hill, ed. (Dedham, 1888), 12 [hereafter Dedham ChR].
18. Dedham ChR, 21.
19. Dedham ChR, 6, 7, 23.
20. Robert Charles Anderson, George F. Sanborn Jr., and Melinde Lutz Sanborn, *The Great Migration: Immigrants to New England, 1634–1635,* Volume V, M–P (Boston 2001), 2:5:170–177.
21. Newbury Town Records, 1:32.

22. *Records of the Colony of New Plymouth in New England*, Nathaniel B. Shurtleff and David Pulsifer, eds., 12 volumes in 10 (Boston, 1855–1861), 12:97, from a deed of 26 December 1643.

23. *Black's Law Dictionary*, rev. 4th ed. (St. Paul, Minn., 1999), 601, 1561.

24. For more detail, see Edward P. Cheyney, "The Manor of East Greenwich in the County of Kent," *The American Historical Review*, 11 (1905–1906):29–35.

25. *Suffolk Deeds* (Boston, 1880), 1:222.

26. *Records and Files of the Quarterly Courts of Essex County, Massachusetts, 1656–1662*, (Salem, 1911–1975), 2:270–271. [hereafter Essex QC]

Chapter Two

1. *The Records of the First Church in Salem, Massachusetts, 1629–1736*, Richard D. Pierce, ed. (Salem, 1974), 16.

2. *Register* 3:40.

3. *The Records of the First Church in Boston, 1630–1868*, Publications of the Colonial Society of Massachusetts, Volumes 39, 40 and 41, Richard D. Pierce, ed. (Boston, 1961), 280 [hereafter Boston ChR].

4. *Winthrop Papers, 1498–1654* (Boston, 1943), 3:283.

5. *Winthrop Papers*, 3:287.

6. *Great Migration Newsletter*, 2:17–18, 24, 3:4–6.

7. Essex QC, 2:389.

8. *Register*, 3:401.

9. Medical Journals of John Winthrop Jr., 1657–1669, manuscript, Massachusetts Historical Society, Boston, 58.

Chapter Three

1. Middlesex County, Mass., Deeds, 6:383.

2. Robert Charles Anderson, *The Great Migration Begins: Immigrants to New England, 1620–1633* (Boston, 1995), 2072.

3. Boston ChR, 14.

4. Richard LeBaron Bowen, *Early Rehoboth: Documented Historical Studies of Families and Events in This Plymouth Colony Township*, 3:126; *The American Genealogist*, 67:35.

5. Suffolk Deeds, 3:413–415.

6. Suffolk Deeds, 6:238–239.

7. Suffolk Deeds, 1:206.

8. Suffolk Deeds, 13:131.

9. Essex QC, 2:389, 5:360, 6:39, 9:345.

10. Essex QC, 5:360.

11. Essex QC, 9:345.

12. Winthrop Medical Journals, 58, 85, 98, 115, 151.

13. Winthrop Medical Journals, 58.

14. *Register*, 3:401; Section One in *Watertown Records Comprising the First and Second Books of Town Proceedings* . . . (Watertown, 1894), 1:32, 1:40; Middlesex County Court Files, Folio 17.

Chapter Four

1. For further details on this case, see *The Genealogist,* 1 (1980):72–79.

Chapter Five

1. *Register,* 23:135–136.
2. *Register,* 30:26–28.
3. *Register,* 131:173–174.
4. *Boston Births, Baptisms, Marriages, and Deaths, 1630–1699,* Ninth Report of the Boston Record Commissioners (Boston, 1883; rpt. Baltimore, 1978), 115. [hereafter Boston VR]
5. Boston VR, 123.
6. Boston VR, 132.
7. *The History of Peter Parker and Sarah Ruggles of Roxbury, Mass., and Their Ancestors and Descendants* (Boston, 1913), 299–301. [hereafter *Parker-Ruggles*]
8. Suffolk County, Massachusetts, Probate Records, 5:300. [hereafter Suffolk PR]
9. Suffolk Deeds, 10:100.
10. *Records of the Suffolk County Court, 1671–1680,* Publications of the Colonial Society of Massachusetts, vol. 30 (Boston, 1933), 849.
11. *Parker-Ruggles,* 301.
12. Suffolk PR, 11:221.
13. *Register,* 131:173–174.
14. "A Volume Relating to the Early History of Boston Containing the Aspinwall Notarial Records from 1644 to 1651," in *Reports of the Record Commissioners of the City of Boston,* Volume 32 (Boston 1903), 18.
15. Essex County, Mass., Deeds, 1:30.
16. [Massachusetts] Supreme Judicial Court, Case #24440.
17. For other examples of this phenomenon, see "The Non-existent William Child of Watertown" (*The American Genealogist,* 62:29–30); "John Black of Charlestown Was Really Robert Blott" (*The American Genealogist,* 67:67–68); and "William Ballard Is Really William Bullard" (*The American Genealogist,* 72:135–136).

Chapter Six

1. For more about Aspinwall and his recordkeeping, see my "Editor's Effusions," *Great Migration Newsletter* 18:10.
2. *Genealogy Standards: Millennium Edition* (2000), 2–8. (This publication has been revised and published as *Genealogy Standards: 50th Anniversary Edition* [2014]).

Chapter Seven

1. *The Probate Records of Essex County, Massachusetts, 1635–1681,* 2:380–381.
2. Essex Deeds, 23:56.
3. *The Great Migration,* 2:2:493–494.
4. Essex QC, 2:42.
5. Essex PR, 1:108–9; Essex QC, 1:168–169.
6. Essex QC, 4:3.
7. See *The Great Migration,* 2:2:171–172. Ralph Farnum and George Varnum are the only known early immigrants of either surname to New England. The only other

known early New England immigrants for these surnames are John Farnham of Dorchester and Henry Farnham of Roxbury, who have not been studied in any detail in this context. However, cursory examination of secondary sources indicates that both were too young to have been father of the wife of Abraham Tyler. James Savage, *A Genealogical Dictionary of the First Settlers of New England*, 4 volumes (Boston, 1860–1862; rpt. Baltimore, 1965), 2:142 [hereafter Savage]; *The American Genealogist*, 62:33–40.

8. This example is derived from unpublished research of David Curtis Dearborn, FASG, Senior Genealogist Emeritus at NEHGS, who has been compiling a Dearborn genealogy for the last four decades.

9. New London Vital Records 1:3.

10. New London Town Records, cited in Frances Manwaring Caulkins, *History of New London, Connecticut* (New London 1895), 144.

11. *The Record of Births, Marriages and Deaths . . . in the Town of Dedham*, Volumes 1 & 2 . . . , Don Gleason Hill, ed. (Dedham, 1886), 1 [hereafter Dedham VR].

12. Dedham VR, 1.

13. Dedham ChR, 21.

14. Dedham ChR, 21.

15. Suffolk PR, 6:43.

16. Some of the arguments given here are presented elsewhere in more detail, with additional evidence bearing on the problem; see *Register*, 130:35–39, and *Great Migration*, 2:3:36–42. These sources also argue that the immigrant John Borden, his wife Joanna, and two older children, born in old England, came to New England in 1635 from Benenden, Kent, as passengers on the *Elizabeth and Anne*. More recently, Eldon Wilson Gay and Christopher Challender Child (*Register*, 164:114–120) have identified Joanna as daughter of Robert Hooker of Lenham, Kent, thus completing her genealogical definition and leading to her full designation as Joanna (Hooker) (Borden) Gay.

17. Savage, 2:368.

18. *A Digest of the Early Connecticut Probate Records, Volume One, Hartford Probate District, 1635–1700*, Charles William Manwaring, comp. (Hartford, 1904), 1:320.

19. Buell Burdett Bassett, *One Bassett Family in America . . .* (Springfield, Mass., 1926), 391; Ernest Flagg, *Genealogical Notes on the Founding of New England: My Ancestors' Part in that Undertaking* (n.p., 1926; rpt. Baltimore, 1973), 258.

20. 12 December 1664 entry: Winthrop Medical Journals, 579; 25 November 1665 entry: Winthrop Medical Journals, 608; 24 December 1665 entry: Winthrop Medical Journals, 611; 14 February 1665/6 entry: Winthrop Medical Journals, 624; 31 March 1666 entry: Winthrop Medical Journals, 637; 18 April 1666 entry: Winthrop Medical Journals, 646; 21 May 1666 entry: Winthrop Medical Journals, 653; 7 July 1666 entry: Winthrop Medical Journals, 670; 18 May 1667 entry: Winthrop Medical Journals, 725; 4 May 1669 entry: Winthrop Medical Journals, 909.

21. *Early Connecticut Probate Records*, 1:426–427.

22. *The American Genealogist*, 70:162–170.

Chapter Eight

1. *The American Genealogist*, 56:80–82; Suffolk Deeds, 16:346.

2. For further details on this case, see *The Genealogist* 1 (1980):72–79.

3. Savage, 4:515.

4. Savage, 4:515–516.

5. Samuel G. Drake, *Result of Some Researches Among the British Archives for Information Relative to the Founders of New England: Made in the Years 1858, 1859 and 1860* (Boston, 1860; rpt. Boston, 2012), 70.
6. Ipswich, Mass., Town Records, 4 [hereafter Ipswich TR].
7. Ipswich TR, 6.
8. Ipswich TR, 8.
9. Ipswich TR, 32–33.
10. Newbury Town Records, 1:44v.
11. Ipswich Land Records, manuscript, Essex County Courthouse, Salem, Massachusetts, 1:53 [hereafter Ipswich LR].
12. Ipswich LR, 1:146.
13. Essex QC, 7:194.
14. Ipswich LR, 1:37, 2:120.
15. Ipswich LR, 5:405.
16. *The American Genealogist*, 57:50–54.
17. *The Great Migration*, 2:7:342–350.
18. I published the discovery of the English origin of John Hunting in 1990 in *National Genealogical Society Quarterly* 78:85-97. I first presented the White Queen Test in 1991 at the International Society for British Genealogy and Family History luncheon in Portland, Oregon, a transcript of which was published in the January–March 1992 issue of *ISBGFH Newsletter.*

Appendix C

1. These statements are from the first page of the Lexicon Working Group's final report, "GENTECH Genealogical Data Model, Phase 1: A Comprehensive Data Model for Genealogical Research and Analysis," published 29 May 2000 and available at ngsgenealogy.org/cs/GenTech_Projects.

Appendix D

1. Arthur Pierce Middleton and Douglass Adair, "The Mystery of the Horn Papers," *The William and Mary Quarterly*, Third Series, 4 (1947):409–445. A brief item summarizing the committee report appeared in the 3 November 1947 issue of *Time* magazine, 47.
2. *Provincial Papers: Documents and Records Relating to the Province of New Hampshire from 1686 to 1722*, 40 volumes, Nathaniel Boulton, ed. (Manchester, N.H., 1867), 1:63–102 [hereafter New Hampshire PP].
3. Sybil Noyes, Charles Thornton Libby, and Walter Goodwin Davis, *Genealogical Dictionary of Maine and New Hampshire* (Portland, Maine, 1928–1939; rpt. Boston, 2011), 8.
4. New Hampshire PP 1:83–86.
5. John Winthrop, *The History of New England from 1630 to 1649*, James Savage, ed., 2 volumes (Boston, 1853). Citations herein refer to the pagination of the 1853 and not the 1826 edition, even though the index to the 1853 edition continues to use the 1826 pagination. 1:500.
6. *Great Migration Newsletter*, 2:30.

Subjects

parish registers containing, 6

record density of, 78

as source material, 1

Middlesex County, Massachusetts, Court files, 29–31

mortgage transactions

formulas used in creating, 17–18

names

chronological list of occurrences of, 124

personal style of recorder of, 3, 15, 16–17, 97, 99, 99

problem resolution and study of, 114

similarity of, 90–94, 116–125

newspapers, marriage records in, 7–8

North Carolina Research: Genealogy and Local History, 2nd ed. (Leary and Stirewalt), 77

nuncupative wills, 27

Oath of Fidelity, 30, 51, 52, 53

onomastics, 114

oral wills, 27

original, meaning of term, 3

original or copy question, 3–11

birth, baptismal, and probate records example for, 8–10

census records example for, 5–6

church records example for, 6–7

Essex Quarter Courts case study for, 19–20

marriage records example for, 7–8

meaning of original in, 3

multiple copies of source and, 4, 10–11

reliability and, 3–4

Shannon's theorem on deterioration in the copier process and, 3–4

vital records example for, 4–5

Winthrop Medical Journal case study for, 20

paradigms, 135–138

parish registers. *See* church records

passenger lists, as sources, 1, 88, 118–119

perpetual calendars, 25, 27

points of comparison

definition of, 132

linkage analysis using, 36–37, 38

possible confidence level, 37

private diaries, as sources, 2, 24

probable confidence level, 37

probates

different jurisdictions and differences in, 3

multiple copies of, 4, 10–11

original or copy question on, 9–10

record density of, 78, 79

source analysis of, 3

as source material, 1, 3

stemmata example of, 10–11

problem analysis

Abigail Powell example of, 68–71

definition of, 132

genealogical phantoms and, 71, 73

Jose Glover example of, 66–68

problem-solving sequence using, xiii, xiv, 65–73

steps of, 65–66

Stephen Farr example of, 71–73

problem resolution

associations in, 114, 115

criteria of, 109–111

definition of, 132

problem-solving sequence using, xiii, xiv–xv, 109–127

Samuel Gay case study for, 111–116, 117

White Queen Test and, 125–127

William White case study for, 116–125

problem selection

Anna Dewey case study for, 59–61

definition of, 132

problem selection *cont.*

genealogically defined concept and, 58–59

partial genealogical networks and, 57–58

problem-solving sequence using, xiii, xiv, 57–63

Samuel Gay case study for, 61–62

problem-solving sequence, xii, xiii–xv

steps in, xiii

provider of information. *See* who provided information question

questions in record analysis, 24, 33

when created question in, 24–26

who created question in, 26

who provided information question in, 26–27

questions in source analysis, 3, 22

original or copy question in, 3–11

what formulas used in creating the source question in, 17–18

when created question in, 11–15

who created question in, 15–17

rationale

constructing, 38

definition of, 35, 132

graphic description of, 36

synthesis and, 83

record, xiii. *See also* Documentation of Records

accurately reported, xii, xiv, 75, 79–80

carefully documented, xii, xiv, 75, 79, 80–81

definition of, 1, 23, 132

document versus, 3

linkage analysis using, 35, 36

reliability of, 2–3

substance of, 2

types of, 23–24

record analysis, xii, xiii, xiv, 23–33

census records example in, 26–27

definition of, 132

discrepant records example in, 25–26

external knowledge used in, 27–28

First Fundamental Rule and, 1

John Borden–Middlesex Court files case study in, 29–31

John Horne–Essex Quarter Courts case study in, 28–29

linkage analysis and, 23, 38, 47

missing dates example in, 24–25

nuncupative (oral) wills example in, 27

questions addressed to, 23, 33

reliability and, 24, 26, 28

source analysis and, 1, 3, 23

substance and, 24, 28

synthesis using, 99

when created question in, 24–26

who created question in, 26

who provided information question in, 26–27

Rachel Hart–Winthrop Medical Journal case study in, 31–32

record creator. *See* who created record question

record density

data collection and, 75, 77–79

definition of, 132

linkage analysis and, 53

synthesis and, 104

variables in, 77–78

recorder

personal style of, 3, 15, 16–17, 97, 99, 99

reliability of, 15–16

record linkage. *See* **linkage analysis**

registers of a church

as source material, 1

reliability

definition of, 2–3, 132

original or copy question and, 3–4

record analysis and, 24, 26, 28

Shannon's theorem on deterioration in the copier process and, 3–4

when created question and, 11

who created question and, 15, 26

Researcher's Guide to American Genealogy, The (Greenwood), 76

resolution. *See* problem resolution

reverse linkage analysis, xiv, 65–66, 69, 72–73

scientific model, 136–137

Second Fundamental Rule, viii, xii, xiii, 35, 54, 110, 111, 116, 127, 132

senior (Sr.), in New England records, 46, 47

ship passenger lists, as sources, 1, 88, 118–119

similarity of names, 90–94, 116–125

source, xiii

  definition of, 1, 143

  document versus, 3

  range of, 1–2

  reliability of, 2–3

  substance of, 2

Source: A Guidebook of American Genealogy, The (Eakle and Cerny), viii, 76

source analysis, xii, xiii, xiv, 1–22

  birth, baptismal, and probate records example for, 8–10

  census records example for, 5–6

  church records example for, 6–7

  comparing all available records in, 12–13

  contemporaneous records with later entries and, 12

  deeds example for, 17–18

  definition of, 133

  discrepant records and, 25–26

  First Fundamental Rule and, 1

  forged documents and, 4

  independent evidence used in, 13–14

  John Horne–Essex Quarter Courts case study in, 19–20

  linkage analysis using, 38, 47

  list analysis and, 14–15

  literary-historical analytic approach in, 2–3

  marriage records example for, 7–8

  mortgage transactions example for, 18

  multiple copies of source and, 4, 10–11

  original or copy question in, 3–11

  questions addressed to, 3, 22

  Rachel Hart–Winthrop Medical Journal case study in, 20–21, 49–50

  record analysis and, 1, 3, 23

  recorder's personal style and, 16–17

  recorder's reliability and, 15–16

  reliability in, 2–3

  substance in, 2

  vital records example for, 4–5

  what formulas used in creating the source question in, 17–18

  when created question in, 11–15

  who created question in, 15–17

source citations

  clarity in, 80

  consistency in, 80

  data collection with, 80–81

specific external knowledge

  data collection and, 75, 76–77

  definition of, 133

  legal model and, 136

  linkage analysis using, 38, 47, 52–53

  record analysis using, 27, 30

  synthesis using, 95

stemmata

  definition of, 10

  probate records example of, 10–11

substance

  definition of, 2, 133

  record analysis and, 24, 28

INDEX
Names

OTHER NEHGS TITLES BY
ROBERT CHARLES ANDERSON, FASG

The Great Migration Begins
Immigrants to New England,
1620–1633 (first series)

6 x 9, 2,386 pp. in 3 vols.

hdcvr, $125; pbk, $79.95

The Great Migration
Immigrants to New England,
1634–1635 (second series)

6 x 9, hdcvr
Vols. I–VII, $59.95–$64.95 per volume

The Pilgrim Migration
Immigrants to Plymouth Colony, 1620–1633

6 x 9 pbk, 708 pp., $29.95

The Winthrop Fleet
Massachusetts Bay Company Immigrants to New England,
1629–1630

6 x 9 hdcvr, 912 pp., $64.95